Icons in Graphics Mode	Icons in Text Mode	Purpose
U	U	Toggles single underlining from a range.
U	U	Toggles double underlining from a range.
$	$	Toggles between currency and global format.
0,0	0,0	Toggles between comma and global format.
%	%	Toggles between percent and global format.
▢	▢	Toggles drop shadow and range outline.
▢	▢	Toggles a range outline on or off.
▒	###	Adds or removes light shading from a range.
ᴬA	²→2	Cycles through available fonts in the current font set.
▨	A→A	Selects the next available color for data in the current range.
ĀA	A→A	Selects the next available color for a range's background.
▦	COPY	Specifies the range to which to copy the current range.
▤	MOVE	Specifies the range to which to move the current range.
≡	←L	Sets label alignment to Left.
≡	←C→	Sets label alignment to Center.
≡	R→	Sets label alignment to Right.
ᴬz	A→Z	Sorts a database in ascending order.

Computer users are not all alike.
Neither are SYBEX books.

We know our customers have a variety of needs. They've told us so. And because we've listened, we've developed several distinct types of books to meet the needs of each of our customers. What are you looking for in computer help?

If you're looking for the basics, try the **ABC's** series. For a more visual approach, select full-color **Teach Yourself** books.

Learn Fast! books are two books in one: a fast-paced tutorial, followed by a command reference.

Mastering and **Understanding** titles offer you a step-by-step introduction, plus an in-depth examination of intermediate-level features, to use as you progress.

Our **Up & Running** series is designed for computer-literate consumers who want a no-nonsense overview of new programs. Just 20 basic lessons, and you're on your way.

SYBEX **Encyclopedias**, **Desktop References**, and **A to Z** books provide a *comprehensive reference* and explanation of all of the commands, features, and functions of the subject software.

Sometimes a subject requires a special treatment that our standard series don't provide. So you'll find we have titles like **Advanced Techniques, Handbooks, Tips & Tricks,** and others that are specifically tailored to satisfy a unique need.

You'll find SYBEX publishes a variety of books on every popular software package. Looking for computer help? Help Yourself to SYBEX.

For a complete catalog of our publications:

SYBEX

SYBEX Inc.
2021 Challenger Drive, Alameda, CA 94501
Tel: (510) 523-8233/(800) 227-2346 Telex: 336311
Fax: (510) 523-2373

SYBEX is committed to using natural resources wisely to preserve and improve our environment. This is why we have been printing the text of books like this one on recycled paper since 1982.

This year our use of recycled paper will result in the saving of more than 15,300 trees. We will lower air pollution effluents by 54,000 pounds, save 6,300,000 gallons of water, and reduce landfill by 2,700 cubic yards.

In choosing a SYBEX book you are not only making a choice for the best in skills and information, you are also choosing to enhance the quality of life for all of us.

Lotus 1-2-3 Release 2.3 & 2.4 for DOS Instant Reference

Lotus 1-2-3® Release 2.3 & 2.4 for DOS® Instant Reference

SECOND EDITION

Judd Robbins

SYBEX®

San Francisco • Paris • Düsseldorf • Soest

Acquisitions Editor: Dianne King
Series Editor: James A. Compton
Editor: Savitha Varadan
Technical Editor: Mark Taber
Word Processor: Susan Trybull
Series Book Designer: Ingrid Owen
Production Artist: Lisa Jaffe
Screen Graphics: Arno Harris
Desktop Publishing Specialist: Thomas Goudie
Proofreader/Production Assistant: Catherine Mahoney
Indexer: Ted Laux
Cover Designer: Archer Design

Screen reproductions produced with Collage Plus.

To Lin

Acknowledgments

These people, who helped so much in the development and production of this book, might go completely unnoticed by the reading public were it not for this solitary book page. Thanks to Jim Compton, series editor; Savitha Varadan, editor; Mark Taber, technical editor; Susan Trybull, word processor; Lisa Jaffe, production artist; Thomas Goudie, desktop publishing specialist; Arno Harris, screen graphics technician; Catherine Mahoney, proofreader; and Ted Laux, indexer. Thanks are also due to SYBEX's acquisitions manager, Dianne King.

Table of Contents

Part III

Using the 1-2-3 Functions

Appendix

Glossary of Macro Keywords

Introduction

Keep this book near your computer. It contains brief yet complete information about every 1-2-3 command, function, macro keyword, and Add-In program included with your 1-2-3 program, both Versions 2.3 and 2.4. You can find solutions quickly to virtually every problem you'll encounter in Lotus 1-2-3. Easy-to-follow examples are included as well to help you understand precisely how the program works.

Quick answers are the essence of this book. Because the information is organized and alphabetized for easy reference, you won't lose time wading through a lot of text. Each command, function, Add-In, and macro is briefly explained. Where appropriate, realistic examples demonstrate how to correctly and effectively use a particular 1-2-3 feature.

This book will be equally useful for Versions 2.3 and 2.4, which do not differ significantly. Version 2.4 offers two new Add-In programs, Backsolver and SmartIcons, as well as a SmartPics feature, which provides a number of ready-made graphic files that you can add to your worksheet. Version 2.4 also offers the capability of printing in landscape mode on *all* printers that 1-2-3 supports, the ability to send output to Encapsulated PostScript (EPS) files, and an improvement of the conversion ability of the Translate utility.

How This Book Is Organized

This book is divided into three parts and one appendix, each designed to help you be a better, more confident user of 1-2-3.

In Part I, read or refresh your memory about the most fundamental aspects of 1-2-3. You will find explanations of how to define a range with either the keyboard or the mouse, and how to access and navigate the 1-2-3 or WYSIWYG menus. Among other fundamental tasks, you can read about the distinction between absolute and relative addressing, as well as the basics of database management.

If you forget the exact syntax of a command, look it up in Part II. Every first- and second-level menu choice is presented alphabetically in this part. You can read step-by-step instructions for running all 1-2-3 commands. Each command entry includes a definition as well as tips, insights, and suggestions for its best and most effective use. All but the most obvious commands also include realistic business, personal, or scientific examples. Where third-level menus and capabilities exist, they are explained and guidance is given for completing all subsequent steps. In Part II you'll also find explanations for attaching and invoking Add-In programs. Entries for Add-In programs include information about each command possibility.

Part III offers definitions and alphabetized entries for all 1-2-3 functions. Cautionary notes and advice for using functions efficiently and correctly are included, as are actual examples of how to use each function.

The appendix provides a glossary of macro keywords. Each macro keyword is defined along with its required syntax and any optional parameters.

On the inside front and back covers of this book you'll find particularly useful information in an easy-access format. This information includes such often-referenced data as the 1-2-3 and WYSIWYG function key assignments, label prefixes, data editing keystrokes, and cell pointer movement keystrokes.

Typographical and Instructional Conventions

If you are following along with the examples in this book and you see boldface text, type the boldface text exactly as it appears. Typically, macro keywords, function names, and menu commands appear in boldface. When an argument requires input, the syntactical placeholder in the book appears in italics. Square brackets appear around optional data or parameters.

In this book, you will see the carriage return symbol (↵). If your keyboard has an Enter or Return key, just press it when you see ↵ in the example instructions in this book.

Part I

The Basics of Lotus 1-2-3

This first Part of the *1-2-3 Instant Reference* introduces you to the overall functionality of the Lotus software. Each of the Main menu choices is explained, and second-level choices are briefly summarized. (Part II explains the major operational choices under each of 1-2-3's Main Menu options.) This Part also explores the 1-2-3 environment in which you'll be doing much of your work. For instance, it explains how to move the cell pointer with the keyboard or the mouse, how to specify and use ranges in many commands, the difference between absolute and relative cell addresses, and the mechanics of and rules associated with using 1-2-3 functions. Refer to this Part as necessary when you are reading about an individual feature or function and you need to know more about it.

RUNNING THE LOTUS ACCESS SYSTEM—AND STARTING 1-2-3

The Lotus Access System is a menu program (LOTUS.EXE) that displays the 1-2-3 executable programs. Table I.1 describes each of the programs available through the Lotus Access System.

Table I.1: Options on the Lotus Access System Menu

Menu Title	Task
1-2-3	Perform worksheet chores
PrintGraph	Print graphics
Translate	Convert data files
Install	Customize 1-2-3 for your hardware
Exit	Return to the operating system

2 The Basics of Lotus 1-2-3

Before you start running the Lotus Access System, make sure the current DOS directory is the one that contains your 1-2-3 files. The directory for hard disk users will probably be **C:\123R23** or **C:\123R24**. Floppy disk systems will probably use the A drive to insert all the necessary diskettes.

Now that you're on the right DOS directory, you can start running the Lotus Access System program. Type **LOTUS** at the command prompt. You will see the Lotus Access Menu, shown in Figure I.1.

The 1-2-3 choice on the horizontal menu is the most commonly used, so it is highlighted initially. To start running 1-2-3 itself, you need only press ↵. This displays the startup 1-2-3 worksheet screen in which you'll do most of your work. To select a different Access System choice, highlight the name of the program you want and press ↵. For example, press the → key and then ↵ to select and run the PrintGraph program. This program's Main Menu appears in Figure I.2.

As Figure I.2 indicates, the PrintGraph program offers its own settings and menu options. It lets you customize and print graphs produced by the /Graph command in the 1-2-3 program.

Like the PrintGraph program, the Translate and Install programs on the Lotus Access Menu manage their own chores with individualized

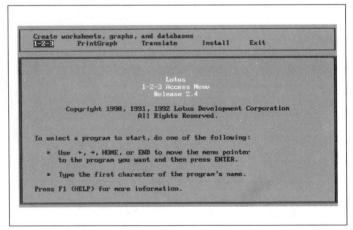

Figure I.1: The Lotus Access Menu

screen displays. Use the Translate utility when you need to convert data formats between 1-2-3 and other software programs. The Translate utility program even enables you to convert data to and from earlier releases of 1-2-3 itself. Its Main Menu screen appears in Figure I.3.

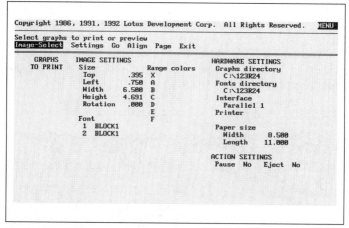

Figure I.2: The PrintGraph Main Menu

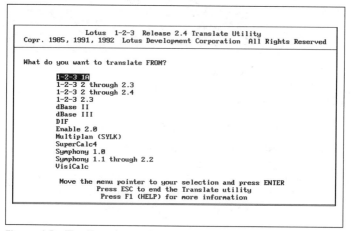

Figure I.3: The Translate utility Main Menu

Use the Install program when you first prepare the 1-2-3 software for use and when you purchase new hardware for your system. When you replace or add monitors, printers, or plotters, you must tell 1-2-3 about your new hardware via the Install program. Figure I.4 shows Install's Main Menu screen.

Selecting Exit on the Lotus Access menu returns you to the DOS prompt, unless you are running 1-2-3 in the OS/2 operating system, or as a separate task within the Windows environment. In those cases, you will return to the appropriate OS/2 system prompt or Windows display. Also, if you installed LOTUS.EXE as one choice of several on a separate menu program, selecting **Exit** returns you to that menu display.

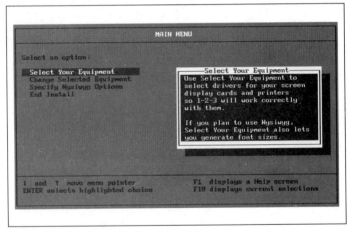

Figure I.4: The Install utility Main Menu

OVERVIEW OF LOTUS 1-2-3

Lotus 1-2-3 is often called an electronic spreadsheet, because of its similarity to an accountant's ledger. On screen, you see a two-dimensional array of numbered rows and lettered columns. In fact, the entire array of 1-2-3's 256 columns by 8192 rows is called a *worksheet*. You can do much more than just number crunching in a 1-2-3 worksheet.

The intersection of each column and each row is called a *cell*, and each cell is tantamount to a mini-calculator. You can move a screen highlight, known as the *cell pointer*, to any specific cell by referencing its address. This *cell identifier* consists of a column letter and row number, such as G14, for example, which represents the cell at the intersection of column G and row 14.

In order to perform calculations or process numeric or text data, you enter numbers, text labels, and sometimes formulas into the worksheet. In any cell you can store numbers or formulas that evaluate to numbers. These are known as 1-2-3 *values*. Alternately, you can store text strings, enclosed in quotation marks, or formulas that evaluate to text strings. These are known as 1-2-3 *labels*. Since virtually all business, scientific, and personal work done with computers consists of either numbers or strings, these two fundamental types of information allow you to customize 1-2-3 to nearly any chore.

To perform accounting tasks, you enter some principal numbers, some dependent formulas, and a few identifying labels in your worksheet. *Voila!* 1-2-3 does the hard part. You've built your own electronic spreadsheet.

To perform database management chores, you enter a few identifying column headings, data to manage in some of the columns, and probably some formulas in other columns. *Voila!* You have a personalized database management facility.

To perform graphic manipulations, and to pretty up your screen and printed output, you enter your numbers, formulas, and labels in appropriate cells. Then, you use the 1-2-3 graphics capability and the WYSIWYG Add-In program to apply fonts, colors, and manage the printed combination of graphics, numbers, and text. *Voila!* You have a unique desktop publishing program that works exactly how you want it to.

MANAGING THE 1-2-3 SCREEN

All operations take place while the worksheet screen, or some superimposed window, appears before you. Table I.2 summarizes the keys you can use while editing your worksheet, and Table I.3 summarizes the keys you can use to control the movement of the 1-2-3 and WYSIWYG cell pointer.

Table I.2: 1-2-3 Data Editing Keys

Key	Meaning
↵	Store the entry and finish editing
→	Move the cursor right one character
←	Move the cursor left one character
↑	Store the entry and move the cell pointer up one row
↓	Store the entry and move the cell pointer down one row
Ctrl-← *or* Shift-Tab	Move the cursor left five characters
Ctrl-→ *or* Tab	Move the cursor right five characters
PgUp	Store the entry and move the cell pointer up one screen
PgDn	Store the entry and move the cell pointer down one screen
Backspace	Erase a character one position to the left of the cursor
Del	Erase the character at the cursor position
End	Move the cursor to the rightmost character
Home	Move the cursor to the first character
Ins	Toggle between Insert and Overtype mode
Esc	Leave Edit mode
F2	Switch to Label or Value mode
F4	Switch to Cell Addressing mode (relative/absolute/mixed)
F9	Recalculate all worksheet formulas
Alt-F1	Compose non-keyboard characters

Table I.3: 1-2-3 Cell Pointer Movement Keys

Key	Moves the Cell Pointer
→	Right one column
←	Left one column
↑	Up one row
↓	Down one row
PgUp	Up one screen
PgDn	Down one screen
Ctrl-← *or* Shift-Tab	Left one screen
Ctrl-→ *or* Tab	Right one screen
End-←, End-→, End-↓, *or* End-↑	To the next nonblank cell (in the direction of the arrow key) that borders a blank cell or the edge of the worksheet
Scroll-←, Scroll-→, Scroll-↓, *or* Scroll-↑	To the current cell in a new worksheet window of displayed cells
End-Home	To the lower-right corner of active cells
Home	To the upper-left corner of active cells
F5	To an explicitly named cell
F6	To the other screen window

In order to control the appearance of text in cells, you can use a variety of text prefixes. Table I.4 summarizes these prefixes and the control functions they perform. The prefix controls the text appearance in the cell and does not itself appear in the cell.

Table I.5 summarizes the primary functions performed by the first ten function keys. Lotus 1-2-3 does not assign any actions to additional function keys that exist on only some keyboards.

Table I.4: 1-2-3 and WYSIWYG Label Prefixes

Label Prefix	Meaning
'	Left-align label (1-2-3)
"	Right-align label (1-2-3)
^	Center-align label (1-2-3)
\	Repeat characters to fill out the cell
¦	Do not print this row (place the broken vertical character at beginning of the row)
¦	Embedded setup strings follow
""	Right-align label (WYSIWYG)
^	Center-align label (WYSIWYG)
'¦	Fill out the cell evenly (WYSIWYG)

Table I.5: 1-2-3 and WYSIWYG Function Keys

Function Key	Unshifted	Alt + Function Key
F1	Help	Compose
F2	Edit	Step
F3	Name	Run
F4	Abs	Undo
F5	Goto	Learn
F6	Window	
F7	Query	Add-In #1
F8	Table	Add-In #2
F9	Calc	Add-In #3
F10	Graph	Add-In #4

Finally, the upper-right corner of a Lotus 1-2-3 or WYSIWYG screen always displays a single status word, called a *mode indicator*. Table I.6 summarizes all possible mode indicators that may appear at different times when running 1-2-3.

ACCESSING A 1-2-3 MENU OPTION

Once you've selected 1-2-3 on the Lotus Access menu and initiated the main 1-2-3 program, you see the worksheet. Press the slash key (/) to activate the 1-2-3 menu system and view the Main Menu. Another way to view the Main Menu is to move the mouse pointer to the top two lines of your screen—1-2-3 will display the Main Menu automatically. The 1-2-3 Main Menu is shown in Figure I.5.

Lines two and three of your screen display the Main Menu, with line two showing the primary menu choices:

Worksheet Range Copy Move File Print Graph Data
System Add-in Quit

Each of these menu choices represents an action or command. Some choices, such as Worksheet and Graph, bring up submenus that offer more options. Other choices, such as Copy or Move, begin a processing task immediately. Lines two and three—and their menu and submenu choices—are called the *control panel*.

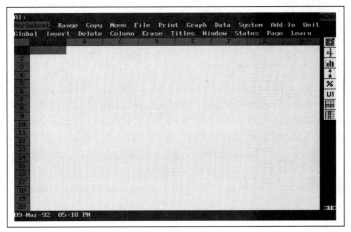

Figure I.5: The Main Menu

Table I.6: Mode Indicators

Color	In WYSIWYG, when you apply Inside, Map, or Background colors with :Graph Edit Color.
Cycle	In WYSIWYG, when switching among graph objects with :Graph Edit Select Cycle.
Drag	In WYSIWYG, when adding a rectangle or ellipse with :Graph Edit Add.
Drivr	In WYSIWYG, when setting a printer driver with :Print Config Printer.
Edit	When editing a cell entry after pressing F2, or after erroneous input.
Error	When an error message appears.
Files	When a list of file or Add-In names appears for selection in the control panel.
Find	When 1-2-3 highlights a matching database entry with the /Data Query Find command.
Frmt	When editing a format line with the /Data Parse Format-Line Edit command.
Help	While a Help screen displays.
Label	When entering a new label.
Menu	When 1-2-3 displays a menu of commands.
Names	When a list of range names or graph names appears in the control panel.
Pan	In WYSIWYG, when adjusting the screen view of a graphic with :Graph Edit View Pan.
Point	When you must enter a range, or when you create a formula by moving the cell pointer.
Ready	When 1-2-3/WYSIWYG is prepared to accept either commands or data.
Select	In WYSIWYG, when choosing objects to apply a common operation to.
Settings	When directly modifying entries in a dialog box.

Table I.6: Mode Indicators (continued)

Size	In WYSIWYG, when changing the size or orientation of objects with :Graph Edit Transform.
Stat	When a worksheet status screen appears.
Text	In WYSIWYG, when editing text directly in cells with :Text Edit.
Value	When entering a value into a cell.
Wait	While 1-2-3/WYSIWYG completes a command or operation.
WYSIWYG	While the WYSIWYG menu appears.

When the Main Menu choice brings up a submenu, the entries on the submenu are displayed on line three. By highlighting each choice on line two of the Main Menu, you can see the subsequent choices displayed on line three. For example, in Figure I.5 Worksheet is highlighted in line two, and line three shows the ten choices that make up the Worksheet submenu.

If you selected the Worksheet choice, 1-2-3 would redisplay the Worksheet submenu on line two of the control panel and you would move down to the second-level of the menu hierarchy. In some cases, selecting a second-level choice, such as Insert, immediately and directly performs a worksheet chore. When a first-level choice (/Worksheet) and a second-level choice (Insert) are combined in this way, they form a single command, in this case the /Worksheet Insert command. Part II of this book offers easy alphabetical access to nearly all of the two-level command combinations.

Sometimes a second-level command merely brings up a third, and, then a fourth, level of menu choices. Part II also discusses and explains these complex commands. You'll find them under the command heading that combines the Main Menu choice with the second-level choice. For example, the /Worksheet Global command displays the following seven choices on a third-level menu:

Format   Label-Prefix   Column-Width   Recalculation
Protection   Default   Zero

You can read about these choices under the /Worksheet Global command in Part II of this book. Table I.7 summarizes the features available through each of 1-2-3's eleven Main Menu choices.

Table I.7: 1-2-3's Main Menu Titles

Menu Title	Task
Worksheet	Manage global and default settings
Range	Manipulate the contents and formats of cell groupings
Copy	Replicate the contents and format of cells
Move	Transfer cell contents and formats to new locations
File	Handle all file manipulations
Print	Produce hard copies or file copies of spreadsheets
Graph	Display data trends graphically
Data	Perform database manipulations on ranges of data
System	Access operating system commands within 1-2-3
Add-in	Connect memory-resident special purpose programs to 1-2-3
Quit	Exit the 1-2-3 program

CONTROLLING PORTIONS, OR RANGES, OF WORKSHEETS

Many 1-2-3 commands affect or act directly on a group or range of cells. The ability to act on cell ranges is fundamental to 1-2-3. A cell range comprises one or more worksheet cells arranged in adjacent rectangular fashion. A range is identified by its starting and ending cell. To tell the program where a range is located, you list the starting cell, a double-period symbol(..), and the ending cell. For example, range G5..G10 is a vertical column of cells, located in column G, beginning at row five and ending at row ten, inclusive. Range B4..F4 is similar but horizontal. It comprises five cells on row four, beginning at column B and ending at column F.

Single-column and single-row ranges are common in 1-2-3 operations. For example, the @SUM function (see Part III) is used frequently to add up a column or row of numbers. But 1-2-3 operations are not limited to single-column or single-row ranges. For example, you could have a larger range, such as E15..G27. In this example, the top-left corner cell (E15) and the bottom-right corner cell (G27) serve to identify a block of 39 cells in a thirteen-row by three-column rectangle.

One last possibility exists. A single cell can constitute a range as well. Any command that acts on a range of cells can also be applied to a single cell. All you have to do is treat the single cell as the simplest of possible ranges, namely a one-by-one rectangle.

To operate on a group of cells, you can use explicit range definitions such as B4..F4 and E15..G27, or you can assign a name to the entire range with the /Range Name command (see Part II). By telling 1-2-3 to act on a named range, you save yourself the time and trouble of having to remember the cell coordinates of its corners. No matter which technique you use, you must at some point define ranges on your worksheet. This can be done with either the keyboard or the mouse.

DEFINING RANGES

Many menu commands require you to enter, or define, a range. When you issue these commands, 1-2-3 switches from Ready to Point mode. At that time, you can complete a range definition by

- typing the column-row coordinates of the range, such as C4..G9;

- using the arrow keys to extend the cell pointer; or

- using the mouse to directly and visually define the range.

Exercise the greatest care when you enter cell ranges by typing their column-row coordinates. With this technique, you can't verify on screen whether the range you entered is correct. On the other hand, when you define a range with the arrow keys or mouse, 1-2-3 expands the cell pointer to display the range in reverse video or in a different color. You can see with a glance what cells are included in the range definition.

Defining a Range with the Keyboard

The general instructions for defining a range are to press any of the four arrow keys to make the range grow or shrink. Simultaneously, the cell coordinates of the range will display automatically on line two of your screen. Press ↵ to complete and lock in the range when you're done highlighting it on-screen.

Suppose that your cell pointer appears at cell B11 and you execute a command like /Range Name. Usually when you begin defining a range, the cell pointer is at one of the four corners of the range you want to define. Before you can begin defining your new range with the keyboard, though, you must press the period key (.) to *anchor* the cell pointer. Line two of your control panel will change from a cell identifier, such as B11, to a range identifier, such as B11..B11. From this moment until you press ↵ to lock in the range, each arrow key press will extend the reverse video highlight or color highlight. Meanwhile, the range definition in the control panel adjusts automatically with each key press. For example, pressing → once makes the range B11..B11 change to B11..C11.

To reset the starting position of a range without having to reissue the /Range Name command, remove the anchor by pressing the Esc key. The range definition on line two will change to a simple cell identifier. Now you can reposition the cell pointer with the arrow keys. Without an anchor, the arrow keys move the single cell pointer; but when a range has an anchor, pressing the arrow keys makes the range definition expand and appear in reverse video or color highlight. When you've reset the cell pointer to the new starting corner cell, press the period key to anchor the range again. Next, highlight the complete block of cells in the range and lock it in by pressing ↵.

Defining a Range with the Mouse

Lotus first introduced mouse controls with Version 2.3. Defining a range with a mouse is notably different from defining a range with the keyboard. The chief difference is that, when a command requests you to enter a range, you can move the mouse pointer anywhere on the screen.

To begin a range definition with the mouse, move the mouse pointer to any corner of the range you want to define. After you have made certain that you are in the right starting cell, press and hold down mouse button one to anchor the range. The cell identifier in line two of the control panel will change to a range identifier. Now move the mouse itself and keep the mouse button depressed. The highlighted range will extend as if you were pressing arrow keys. When you have highlighted the complete range, release the mouse button. Next, click the mouse once to complete the range definition. Clicking the mouse is the equivalent of pressing ↵ to accept and lock in a highlighted range.

If you want to remove the range anchor and reset the starting point of the range, click the second mouse button—typically the right one. The highlighted range will revert to a single cell highlight, and the range definition in line two of the control panel will show a starting cell identifier only. Now you may move the mouse pointer to a new starting point for the range.

RELATIVE AND ABSOLUTE CELL ADDRESSING

1-2-3 commands nearly always act on or in one or more worksheet cells. Since the /Copy and /Move commands are so important and frequently used, the issue of cell addresses is a crucial one. When a formula that refers to a cell or cell range is replicated with the /Copy command or transferred with /Move, questions arise as to which cells the newly located formulas will act on.

To answer this question, and to use the worksheet formulas correctly, you must understand the difference between *relative* and *absolute* cell addresses. Relative addressing is the most common technique and treats cells according to where they are positioned relative to the cell that contains the referencing formula. Absolute addressing, on the other hand, refers to specific cells, regardless of where the referencing formulas are located.

To demonstrate this important difference, let's look at some examples. Suppose that your worksheet automates a point-of-sale cash register operation. The item number of the product being purchased goes in column A, and the quantity being purchased in column B. A formula looks up the unit price of the item and stores it in column C. Finally, another formula calculates the tax for column D. The final column, E, contains the dollar contribution to the total charges for each particular line item.

For example, in row seven, the dollar cost before tax of a particular purchase is obtained by multiplying the item quantity (in B7) by the price per item (in C7). Adding the tax (in D7) produces the final result, and is given by the formula

+B7*C7+D7

Other items sold contribute to the final sales total with comparable formulas in column E:

Cell E8 contains   **+B8*C8+D8**

Cell E9 contains   **+B9*C9+D9**

Cell E10 contains   **+B10*C10+D10**

and so on.

In each case, 1-2-3 calculates the charges in column E by multiplying the value in the cell three columns to the left (the item quantity in column B) by the value in the cell two columns to the left (the unit price in column C), and by adding that product to the value in the cell immediately to the left (the sales tax in column D). This type of addressing is called *relative addressing*, because on each row, each of the cell addresses used in the column E formula is located a relative number of columns to the left of the formula itself. Relative addressing is the default mode for 1-2-3 operations.

A relative address consists of a column letter and a row number. It is always interpreted by looking for a certain cell that is located a relative number of columns and rows away from the current one. Relative addressing works well with copied formulas that rely on information in other cells—on the same row—whose relative position changes along with the current cell. In our example, the formula in each row of the point-of-sale worksheet changed, yet always calculated its results from cell values that were relatively positioned on the same row. As the row changed for the column E formula, both the formula location and the elements of the formula changed to the new row.

But not all formulas act this way. For example, a loan amortization worksheet calculates the payoff amounts on a monthly loan. Let's say, for the first month, cell D12 contains a formula to calculate the interest portion of the loan payment:

+$D$3/12*C12

This formula necessarily refers to cell D3 as cell $D$3. The dollar signs placed in front of both the column D identifier and the row 3 identifier represent *absolute addressing*. When multiple formulas in a worksheet must refer to a single value located in an unchanging cell, such as the annual interest rate in cell D3, absolute addressing becomes essential.

The formula is still evaluated by 1-2-3 by dividing D3's value by 12, then multiplying the result by the entry in cell C12. Typically, this means that the annual interest rate in cell D3 (a fixed location in the worksheet) is divided by 12 to obtain the monthly interest rate, and multiplied by the current month's principal balance in the adjacent cell C12. Each worksheet row represents a different month.

Without the dollar signs, a relative addressing formula would fail when copied to subsequent rows for other months. If the formula entry specified D3 instead of $D$3, the first four formulas might look like this:

Cell Address	Contents
D12	+D3/12*C12
D13	+D4/12*C13
D14	+D5/12*C14
D15	+D6/12*C15

Because cell D12 contains a relative addressing formula, 1-2-3 adjusts the cell references for each subsequently copied formula. D12 is interpreted to consist of a value obtained from a cell in the same column, but nine cells above the current cell, divided by twelve, and multiplied by a value obtained from a cell immediately to the left.

In all subsequent row formulas for different months, you always want the value for annual interest to be obtained from cell D3. Consequently, D3 must be treated as an absolute, unchanging address. No matter where you copy or move a formula that refers to the annual interest rate, you want 1-2-3 to obtain that value from cell D3. Using an absolute address for cell D3, the original formula and the copied formulas would now appear as

Cell Address	Contents
D12	+$D$3/12*C12
D13	+$D$3/12*C13
D14	+$D$3/12*C14
D15	+$D$3/12*C15

Because the cell reference to D3 in the first formula appeared absolutely (as $D$3), 1-2-3 did not modify it when it copied the formula and modified the other (relative) cell reference in column C.

THE BASICS OF DATABASE MANAGEMENT

1-2-3 is not a database manager, but it is often used to manage groups of related data. For example, you could keep track of a company's inventory, storing the name, identification, and price of all stock items. Or you could maintain customer lists, with each entry including a name, address, and phone number. Figure I.6 shows a sample personnel records database comprising the information in cells A3..D9.

Fields and Records

Portions of a database table contain related information. For example, the first row contains the *field names*—the names of data items stored in the database table itself. One field name appears at the top of each column.

One entire column is considered a *field*. A field extends from the column name to the last row in the column in which an entry has been made. For example, in Figure I.6 the NAME field comprises the cells in the range B3..B9. This field, then, includes all the NAME labels in the personnel records database.

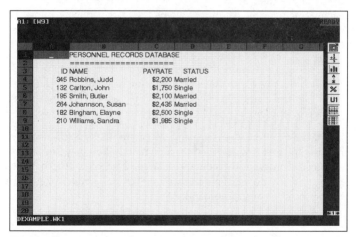

Figure I.6: A personnel records database

Notice that each personnel entry, or row, in the database table includes a group of related information—an ID, a NAME, a PAY-RATE, and a marital STATUS. Groups of related information stored in cells on the same row of a worksheet are called *records*. In Figure I.6, the cell range A7..D7 includes all data about employee Susan Johannson. As such, this information comprises one record.

As you build or manipulate a database table, you can choose the number and kind of fields to include. Each column represents a category of data about a table entry. Usually you'll decide on the kind of entries you want to make before you decide how to divide each entry into rows. Each row, or record, contains related data items, or fields, stored in adjacent cells. To identify each field for 1-2-3 database operations—for menu commands or functions—you will enter a label as the field name in the top row of the table.

Database Design Rules

When you construct 1-2-3 database tables, you must follow certain rules. Doing so ensures a consistent design, and makes it easier for others to work with your data and understand your worksheets.

First, reserve row one of the database table for field names. You can use whatever names you like and left-justify, right-justify, or center each name over the column by using the apostrophe ('), quotation mark ("), or caret (^) prefix symbols respectively. At the very least, however, each name should suggest the contents of the column.

Succeeding rows of the database should contain data records. Do not include any blank rows or separator rows in your database. Some database commands will fail if they encounter unexpected blank row entries.

The largest a worksheet can be is 256 columns by 8,192 rows, including the first row reserved for field names. You may need to use a different program if you manage larger databases. Alternatively, you could divide a large database into several smaller ones, each fitting the size constraints of 1-2-3.

Furthermore, each field name must be unique. 1-2-3 cannot be sure which column you want to use in a formula or function reference if the label used for one field name is the same as the one used for another. Consequently, you may obtain no results, or incorrect results.

Finally, you must decide in advance whether you are storing values or labels in each field. If a field is to contain labels, you must not enter any values into the column. Conversely, if the column is to contain values, do not place any labels in that field's cells.

USING 1-2-3 FUNCTIONS

A *function* is a unique 1-2-3 feature. In one sense, it consists of a series of predetermined instruction steps. In another sense, it acts just like a complex formula that results in a final number or text string. A function is really a sophisticated cross between a simple value and a complex formula. The functions' built-in logic is completely hidden from you, and is performed automatically whenever you refer to a function in a cell formula.

Each function performs a well-defined task—and produces well-defined results. Part III describes and offers examples in how to use each of 1-2-3's many powerful functions. For each function to do its pre-programmed job, it usually requires some input information on which or with which to work. Each function represents a shorthand notation for a specific series of processing steps. In the introduction to Part III, all of 1-2-3's functions are categorized into groups according to the class of task they perform.

Rules for Using Functions

In order to use functions effectively, you must follow certain rules. Each function must begin with an At (@) symbol. This tells 1-2-3 that the succeeding word will be a function name. After the function name, you must include in parentheses all inputs that are necessary for the function to perform its task.

Function inputs, called *arguments*, can be literal values, character strings, or references to cells that contain or compute values or labels. As you read about the various functions in Part III, you will discover what types of inputs each one requires. If a value is required, for example, you can use any of the following for an argument entry:

- The actual number itself in the function's parentheses.

- A cell identifier that specifies where the value can be found.

- A formula that computes the value.

- A formula in a cell that is referred to in the function's argument list. When 1-2-3 calculates the function, it will recalculate the referenced formula.

Similarly, string arguments can be any one of the following entries:

- The actual text string itself, surrounded by quotation marks, in the function's parentheses.

- A cell identifier that specifies where the text label can be found.

- A formula that computes the needed text string.

- A formula in a cell that is referred to in the function's argument list. When 1-2-3 calculates the function, it will recalculate the referenced formula.

Each unique input argument must be separated by a comma from the next argument. When you include a function in a cell, you must follow the function's *syntax*. A function's structure, which consists of the @ symbol, function name, and the required arguments in parentheses, is known as the syntax of the function.

Table I.8 shows a series of sample arguments used in functions.

Table I.8: Sample Arguments Used in Functions

Type	Sample Argument	Meaning
Value	15	The number 15
	C24	The numeric contents of cell C24
	INTEREST	A name of a single-cell range containing a number or numeric formula
	INTEREST/12	A numeric formula
	PRINCIPAL>185000# AND#CREDIT=1	A logical formula that results in a numeric value of 1 (for TRUE) or 0 (for FALSE)
String	"Robbins"	A literal text string
	D24	A cell containing a label or a text formula
	@MID(A1,@FIND(":", A1,0)+1,35)	A string function
	COMPANY	A range name containing a label or another string
	+"Route to "&C3	A string formula

As you practice using the functions presented in Part III, remember these important rules about their syntax:

- Each function has a unique function name preceded by the At sign (@).

- If a function requires arguments, the arguments must be enclosed in parentheses.

- Multiple arguments must be separated by commas (,) or semi-colons (;), although commas are the usual choice for argument separators. (With the /Worksheet Global Default Other International Punctuation command, you can choose other separators, such as periods.)

- Spaces are not allowed between arguments, or on either side of the parentheses.

- Function names can be entered in upper- or lowercase.

- You may *nest* one function within another, but you must take care to use parentheses to group and clarify the different functions' arguments.

UNDOING A MISTAKE

The Undo facility is one of 1-2-3's most powerful features. From time to time, you will make a mistake. Depending on its severity, you may have to retype a single value or an entire worksheet.

By pressing Alt-F4 to activate the Undo command, you can restore the previous status of your worksheet. Whether you accidentally typed over a formula, erroneously jumbled an entire database table, or retrieved a new file and obliterated your worksheet, Undo can rescue you. Pressing Alt-F4 restores your worksheet area to its status at the time the Ready indicator was last showing.

To manage the Undo process, 1-2-3 reserves a portion of memory for storing the most recent copy of the worksheet. When you press Alt-F4, 1-2-3 reads this last version of your worksheet from this special memory area. It overwrites the current worksheet with the preceding version and thereby restores your worksheet to its former state.

If you want Undo to be on, select the /Worksheet Global Default Other Undo Enable command. Unfortunately, the Undo facility consumes a relatively large amount of available memory. However, if you don't need this memory for large worksheets, keeping the Undo facility activated is not a disadvantage. You can disable the Undo feature with the /Worksheet Global Default Other Undo Disable command, but no matter how experienced you become, there will surely come a time when you wish you could press one key to correct a mistake. Therefore, don't disable the Undo feature unless you really have to.

Part II

Using the 1-2-3 Worksheet Operations

THE /ADD-IN ATTACH COMMAND

- **PURPOSE**   To load an Add-In program into memory.

To Select and Load an Add-In Program into Memory:

1. Bring up the Main Menu and select **Add-In**.

2. Select **Attach** from the second-level menu.

3. Select one of the Add-In program names listed on line three of the screen:

AUDITOR.ADN, BSOLVER.ADN, ICONS.ADN, MACROMGR.ADN, TUTOR.ADN, VIEWER.ADN, or WYSIWYG.ADN

4. Later you can run the program you selected by choosing the **/Add-In Invoke** command or by pressing an Alt-function key combination—Alt-F7, Alt-F8, Alt-F9, or Alt-F10. To be able to run an Add-In program with an Alt-function key combination, select the function key number 7, 8, 9, or 10 on the menu that appears. To run an Add-In program with the /Add-In Invoke command instead of an Alt-function key combination, select **No-Key** from this menu.

5. Select **Quit** to return to Ready mode.

- **NOTES**   You can automatically attach a specific Add-In program each time you run 1-2-3. To do so, you must select the **/Worksheet Global Default Other Add-In** command. Next, choose **Set** and specify the Add-In program you want attached automatically. (Choose Cancel if you change your mind and decide to disengage the automatic attachment.) You may attach up to eight Add-In programs automatically each time you start up 1-2-3.

However, before an Add-In program can be attached automatically, you must add its name to 1-2-3's configuration file. Do this by selecting **/Worksheet Global Default Update**. Now, when you start up 1-2-3, the attachment will be performed automatically.

Examples

To load the AUDITOR Add-In program into memory and assign it the APP1 (Alt-F7) designation, choose **/Add-In Attach AUDITOR.ADN 7**. Because the /Add-In menu is still visible on line two, you can load the MACROMGR Add-In program into memory as well and assign it APP2 (Alt-F8) merely by selecting **Attach MACROMGR.ADN 8**. Choose **Quit** to exit from the menu and return to Ready mode.

See Also   /Add-In Detach, /Add-In Invoke, /Add-In Clear, /Add-In Quit, AUDITOR, BSOLVER, ICONS, MACROMGR, TUTOR, VIEWER, WYSIWYG, and /Worksheet Global.

THE /ADD-IN CLEAR COMMAND

● **PURPOSE**   To remove all attached Add-In programs from memory.

To Clear the Add-In Programs You Have Attached:

1.   Bring up the Main Menu and select **Add-In**.

2.   Select **Clear** from the second-level menu.

3.   Select **Quit** to return to Ready mode.

● **NOTES**   Use this command when you want to reclaim the memory being used by one or more Add-In programs and use it instead to store worksheet data or to fit a different Add-In program into memory.

Examples

To reclaim all the memory space currently being used by Add-In programs, select **/Add-In Clear**. If there is no memory to reclaim because no Add-In programs are currently attached, a small dialog box with the words "No Add-Ins attached" will appear in the center of your screen.

See Also /Add-In Attach, /Add-In Detach, /Add-In Invoke, and /Add-In Quit.

THE /ADD-IN
DETACH COMMAND

● **PURPOSE** To remove an already attached Add-In program from memory.

To Select and Clear
an Add-In Program You Have Attached:

1. Bring up the Main Menu and select **Add-In**.

2. Select **Detach** from the second-level menu.

3. Select one of the attached Add-In program names listed on line three.

4. Select **Quit** to return to Ready mode.

● **NOTES** Use this command when you want to reclaim the memory being used by an Add-In program and use it instead to store worksheet data or to fit a different Add-In program into memory.

Examples

To remove the MACROMGR Add-In program and retain other attached Add-Ins in memory, choose **/Add-In Detach MACROMGR**.

See Also   /Add-In Attach, /Add-In Invoke, /Add-In Clear, and /Add-In Quit.

THE /ADD-IN
INVOKE COMMAND

● **PURPOSE**   To execute an already attached Add-In program.

To Select and Run
an Add-In Program You Have Attached:

1. Bring up the Main Menu and select **Add-In**.

2. Select **Invoke** from the second-level menu.

3. Select one of the attached Add-In program names listed on line three.

4. Select **Quit** to return to Ready mode.

● **NOTES**   By assigning an Alt-function key combination to an Add-In program when you attach it, you can run the Add-In without selecting /Add-In Invoke. Instead, press the assigned function key—Alt-F7, Alt-F8, Alt-F9, or Alt-F10—in Ready mode. However, if you attached more than four Add-In programs, and so assigned all four possible Alt-function key combinations, the only way to initiate an additional program is to use the /Add-In Invoke command.

Examples

Suppose you loaded the AUDITOR and MACROMGR Add-In programs into memory with the **/Add-In Attach** command. Now, you can activate AUDITOR by pressing Alt-F7 at the Ready prompt. The AUDITOR's Settings dialog box will appear in the center of the screen, and its Main Menu will appear on line two. Whether or not you assigned the Alt-F7 combination to AUDITOR, you can run it by choosing **/Add-In Invoke AUDITOR**.

To run the MACROMGR, or any other Add-In program, you must return to Ready mode. Next, press MACROMGR's Alt-function key combination, or choose the **/Add-In Invoke** command.

See Also /Add-In Attach, /Add-In Detach, /Add-In Clear, /Add-In Quit, AUDITOR, MACROMGR, TUTOR, VIEWER, and WYSIWYG.

THE AUDITOR ADD-IN

● **PURPOSE** To analyze all logical relationships between worksheet cells and formulas.

To Identify Referenced Cells:

1. Bring up the AUDITOR Main Menu and select **Precedents**.

2. Answer the "Select precedent source cell" query on line two by moving the cell or mouse pointer to the cell with the formula you wish to analyze.

3. Press ↵ or click the mouse to complete the operation. The AUDITOR will identify all cells that influence—or supply data to—the source cell.

4. Depending on the status of Audit mode, take one of the
    following actions:

    a. If Audit mode was Highlight, choose **Quit** to return to
    Ready mode and view the identified, intensified cells.

    b. If Audit mode was List, answer the "Specify range for
    list" prompt by moving the cell pointer to an empty area
    of the worksheet. Press ↵ to complete the operation.
    Choose **Quit** to return to Ready mode and view the cell
    identifiers and contents written into the target range.

    c. If Audit mode was Trace, the first cell referenced by this
    source cell's contents is highlighted, and a new submenu
    with three choices appears on line two:

    • **Forward** moves the block cursor to the next cell, if
    any, that influences the source cell.

    • **Backward** moves the block cursor to the previous cell
    in the chain of cells that influences the source cell.

    • **Quit** returns you to the AUDITOR Main Menu.

To Identify Referencing Formulas:

1. Bring up the AUDITOR Main Menu and select **Dependents**.

2. Answer the "Select dependent source cell" query on line
    two by moving the cell or mouse pointer to the cell with
    the formula you wish to analyze.

3. Press ↵ or click the mouse to complete the operation. The
    AUDITOR will identify all cells that depend on your high-
    lighted source cell.

4. Depending on the status of Audit mode, take one of the
    following actions:

    a. If Audit mode was Highlight, choose **Quit** to return to
    Ready mode and view the identified, intensified cells.

    b. If Audit mode was List, answer the "Specify range for
    list" prompt by moving the cell pointer to an empty area
    of the worksheet. Press ↵ to complete the operation.
    Choose **Quit** to return to Ready mode and view the cell
    identifiers and contents written into the target range.

   c. If Audit mode was Trace, the first cell that depends on your specified source cell is highlighted, and a new sub-menu with three choices appears on line two:

- **Forward** moves the block cursor to the next cell, if any, that depends on the source cell.

- **Backward** moves the block cursor to the previous cell in the chain of cells that depends on the source cell.

- **Quit** returns you to the AUDITOR Main Menu.

To Identify All Formulas:

1. Bring up the AUDITOR Main Menu and select **Formulas**.

2. Depending on the status of Audit mode, take one of the following actions:

   a. If Audit mode was Highlight, choose **Quit** to return to Ready mode and view the identified, intensified cells.

   b. If Audit mode was List, answer the "Specify range for list" prompt by moving the cell pointer to an empty area of the worksheet. Press ⏎ to complete the operation. Choose **Quit** to return to Ready mode and view the cell identifiers and contents written into the target range.

   c. If Audit mode was Trace, the first cell that contains a formula is highlighted, and a new submenu with three choices appears on line two:

- **Forward** moves the block cursor to the next cell, if any, that contains a formula.

- **Backward** moves the block cursor to the previous cell in the range that contains a formula.

- **Quit** returns you to the AUDITOR Main Menu.

The AUDITOR identifies formulas from left to right (columns) and, within each column of the audit range, from top to bottom (rows). This is the forward direction.

To List Formulas by Recalculation Order:

1. Bring up the AUDITOR Main Menu and select **Recalc-List**.

2. Depending on the status of Audit mode, take one of the following actions:

   a. If Audit mode was Highlight, choose **Quit** to return to Ready mode and view the identified, intensified cells.

   b. If Audit mode was List, answer the "Specify range for list" prompt by moving the cell pointer to an empty area of the worksheet. Press ↵ to complete the operation. Choose **Quit** to return to Ready mode and view the cell identifiers and contents written into the target range.

   c. If Audit mode was Trace, the first cell in 1-2-3 recalculation order that contains a formula is highlighted, and a new submenu with three choices appears on line two:

     • **Forward** moves the block cursor to the next cell, if any, that contains a formula.

     • **Backward** moves the block cursor to the previous cell in the range that contains a formula.

     • **Quit** returns you to the AUDITOR Main Menu.

The Recalc-List option directs the AUDITOR to identify cell formulas in recalculation order (set or reset with the /Worksheet Global Recalculation command).

To Identify Circular Cell References:

1. Bring up the AUDITOR Main Menu and select **Circs**. The screen clears, Circs mode is activated, and all circular references are displayed.

2. Press **Esc** to return to the AUDITOR Main Menu.

To Set or Reset the Audit Range:

1. Bring up the AUDITOR Main Menu and select **Options**.

2. Select **Audit-Range** from the second-level menu.

3. Using the keyboard or mouse, identify a range of work-sheet cells to be the subject of Auditing Menu commands you intend to issue.

4. Select **Quit** to return to the AUDITOR Main Menu.

To Set or Reset the Audit Mode:

1. Bring up the AUDITOR Main Menu and select **Options**.

2. To set one of the three possible Audit modes,

   a. Choose **Highlight** to intensify all identified cells.

   b. Choose **List** to write identified cells to the worksheet.

   c. Choose **Trace** to identify each audited cell.

3. Select **Quit** to return to the AUDITOR Main Menu.

The Audit mode you select from the Options menu determines how the AUDITOR presents its findings to you. **Highlight** identifies auditing results by intensifying or changing the color of cells. **List** writes cell names and contents to a specified portion of your worksheet. **Trace** displays a block cursor successively at each cell that meets the auditing criteria.

● **NOTES**   Before you can run the AUDITOR program with the /Add-In Invoke command, you must use the /Add-In Attach menu choice to load AUDITOR into memory. Alternatively, you can run AUDITOR by pressing one of four Alt-function key combinations, provided you made the Alt-function assignment during the /Add-In Attach process.

The AUDITOR scans a portion of your worksheet, called the *Audit-Range*, and in Audit mode identifies all cells that meet your requested criteria. You should set the Audit Range and the Audit mode before you request a Main Menu auditing operations, because if you do not set these values yourself the AUDITOR will use the entire worksheet as the audit range (A1..IV8192) and set the Audit mode to Highlight.

When you set the Audit mode to List, 1-2-3 will ask you for a target range into which the AUDITOR can write its identified cells and formulas. Be sure that this range is both empty and large enough to hold all the possible results.

In Trace mode, you'll hear a beep in both forward and backward directions when no more cells meet the criteria you specified.

If you are using the highlighting method to identify referenced or referencing cells, choose Options Reset Highlight Quit in between Main Menu operations to restore normal display to all cells. This way, you won't be confused by which cells are being highlighted by a current request, and which cells were highlighted by a previous one.

Examples

Suppose, in your worksheet, that column B contained dates entered as textual labels, such as "5/13/52"; that column C converted these dates into date values with the @DATEVALUE function; and that column D used the date values to convert and extract numeric months for other worksheet purposes.

You could identify all referenced cells by turning on List mode for auditing, running the AUDITOR Add-In, and selecting **Options List Quit Precedents**. Next, specify one of the column D functions, say D4, as the source cell to analyze. This cell may contain a simple @MONTH(C4) formula. After you assign a blank portion of your worksheet as a single-column location for the AUDITOR to write the list of cell references and then choose **Quit**, you might see the following result:

Precedents of cell D4

C4: @DATEVALUE(B4)

B4: '5/13/52

See Also   / Add-In Attach, / Add-In Invoke, BSOLVER, ICONS, MACROMGR, TUTOR, VIEWER, and WYSIWYG.

THE BSOLVER ADD-IN (RELEASE 2.4)

● **PURPOSE**   To calculate backwards from a specified formula result to the starting value(s) that produce that result.

To Specify the Cell Containing the Desired Formula Result:

1. From the main BSOLVER menu, select Formula-Cell.

2. In response to the "Enter the range address or name of the formula cell" prompt on line 2, move the cell or mouse pointer to the cell containing the formula whose resulting value you wish to set.

3. Press ↵ or click the mouse to complete the operation.

To Specify the Final Formula Value:

1. From the main BSOLVER menu, select Value.

2. In response to the "Enter the desired result value" prompt on line 2, type the final value that you would like the result formula to have.

3. Press ↵ to complete the operation.

To Specify the Starting Variable(s) to Change:

1. From the main BSOLVER menu, select Adjustable.

2. In response to the "Enter the range address or name of the adjustable cell" prompt on line 2, move the cell or mouse pointer to the cell or range of cells that contain values that Backsolver can change.

3.   Highlight the desired cell or range of cells, then press ↵ or click the mouse to complete the operation. Alternatively, you can type in a cell name, cell range, or valid range name, then press ↵.

To Solve for the Desired Starting Value(s):

1.   First, create a worksheet that contains an appropriate formula, and all necessary starting values in other cells.

2.   Invoke the Backsolver Add-In and use the Formula-Cell choice to specify the cell containing the desired formula result.

3.   Choose Value and enter the desired final value of the specified formula.

4.   Choose Adjustable to specify one or more cells that contain starting values used by the specified formula.

5.   Choose Solve. Backsolver will compute adjusted value(s) for the starting variables in the cell(s) specified as adjustable.

● **NOTES**   You must first use the /Add-In Attach menu choice to load BSOLVER into memory. Then, you can run the program with the /Add-In Invoke command. Alternatively, you can press one of four possible function key combinations, if you specified the specific assignment during the /Add-In Attach process. Select Quit to return to READY mode. BSOLVER is only available in 1-2-3 Release 2.4.

Only the top-left corner of a cell range is used as the Formula Cell, if anything other than a single cell is specified. When entering a value, you can type a formula that depends on existing worksheet values and cell contents. 1-2-3 will immediately evaluate the formula you enter and use the resulting value, as though you had computed it yourself and then entered it in response to the "desired result value" prompt.

When you specify the adjustable cell(s), you can enter a single cell, a cell range, or a valid range name. Only unprotected values are

adjusted by Backsolver. Protected cells in a range are not affected.
Neither are blank cells, or cells containing text strings or other formulas. If you do enter a range of cells to be adjusted, Backsolver
will adjust all specified cells by the same proportional amount; this
is called *proportional backsolving*.

● **EXAMPLES**   Suppose that you want to make an offer that you
can afford to a car dealer. His car lists for $20,000. You have $5,000
available for a down payment, leaving $15,000 to finance at the avail-
able rate. In a conventional worksheet, you could use the @PMT
formula to calculate how much of a monthly payment that car would
involve. On a five-year loan at ten percent interest, you could store
15000 in cell B1, 10% in cell B2, and 60 (months) in cell B3. The formula @PMT(B1,B2/12,B3) in cell B5, for instance, would result in a
monthly payment of $318.71.

However, suppose that you could only afford a monthly payment
of $250. You can use the Backsolver Add-In to work backwards to a
purchase price you can afford. Invoke the BSOLVER add-in and set
Formula-Cell to cell B5, the cell that contains the formula whose
resulting value you wish to specify. Then choose Value and type in
the desired result of 250. Next, choose Adjustable and specify cell B1,
the cell containing the value that you wish Backsolver to adjust.

When you finally select the Solve choice, Backsolver will adjust cell B1
as necessary to ensure that the formula in cell B5 results in a value
of $250. Specifically, this results in $11,766 for cell B1, which means
that you could have your $250 monthly payment if you were able
to convince the dealer to accept about $16,000 for his $20,000 car.
This price would leave you $766 for miscellaneous charges after a
$5,000 down payment.

See Also   /Add-In Attach, /Add-In Invoke, ICONS, MACRO-
MGR, TUTOR, VIEWER, WYSIWYG

THE /COPY COMMAND

● **PURPOSE**   To replicate one or more cells in a different portion of the worksheet.

To Copy One Cell to Another:

1.   Move the cell pointer to the cell you wish to copy.

2.   Bring up the Main Menu and select **Copy**.

3.   Answer the "Copy What?" prompt by pressing ↵ or clicking the mouse to accept the highlighted, or source cell, as the one to copy.

4.   Move the cell pointer to the target cell, the one to which you want to copy the first cell.

5.   Press ↵ or click the mouse to complete the operation.

Once the Copy operation is complete, 1-2-3 returns the cell pointer to the source cell. Not only the contents, but the formatting of the source cell is copied to the target cell.

To Copy One Cell to a Range of Other Cells:

1.   Move the cell pointer to the cell you wish to copy.

2.   Bring up the Main Menu and select **Copy**.

3.   Answer the "Copy What?" prompt by pressing ↵ or clicking the mouse to accept the highlighted, or source cell, as the one to copy.

4.   Move the cell pointer to any corner of the target range, the range of cells to which you want to make copies of the source cell.

5.   Highlight the entire range of target cells.

6.   Press ↵ or click the mouse to complete the operation.

After the Copy operation is complete, 1-2-3 returns the cell pointer to the source cell. Not only the contents, but the cell formatting of the source cell is copied to all the cells in the highlighted range of target cells.

To Copy an Entire Range of Cells to Another Worksheet Location:

1.   Move the cell pointer to any corner of the range of cells you wish to copy.

2.   Bring up the Main Menu and select **Copy**.

3.   Answer the "Copy What?" prompt by highlighting the entire range of cells you want to copy. Press ↵ or click the mouse to accept this block of cells as the source cells for copying.

4.   Move the cell pointer to the upper-left corner of the target range, the range of cells to which you want to make copies of the source cells. The target range extends down and to the right of the cell you specify.

5.   Press ↵ or click the mouse to complete the operation.

After the Copy operation is complete, 1-2-3 returns the cell pointer to the cell-range corner you specified in step 1 to begin the copying procedure. Not only the contents, but the formatting of the original cells is copied to the cells in the target area.

● **NOTES**   Use the /Copy command to save the time and effort of having to reenter formulas, labels, or values in other portions of your worksheet. 1-2-3 automatically adjusts all relative references found in formulas in the copied cells.

Use other 1-2-3 commands for specialized copying operations. For example, to import a range of cells from a disk-based worksheet into the current worksheet, use the /File Combine command. To copy a range of cells from the current worksheet to a separate worksheet file on disk, use the /File Xtract command. If you need to copy the contents of a row of cells into a column, or vice versa, use the /Range Trans command. To copy resulting values only, rather than the original formulas, use the /Range Value command.

Examples

To copy the contents and formatting of cell A5 to F13, move the cell pointer to A5, bring up the Main Menu, and select **Copy**. Press ↵ or click the mouse to accept A5 as the source cell, and move the cell pointer to F13. Press ↵ or click the mouse to complete the operation.

To copy the cells in the range C7..D9 to new locations in range F10..G12, first move the cell pointer to C7, bring up the Main Menu, and select **Copy**. Extend the cell pointer to highlight the entire source range C7..D9. Press ↵ or click the mouse to accept this highlighted range as the source. Move the cell pointer to F10 and press ↵ or click the mouse to complete the operation.

See Also   "Defining Ranges" in Part 1, /File Combine, /File Xtract, /Range Trans, and /Range Value.

THE /DATA DISTRIBUTION COMMAND

● **PURPOSE**   To determine how many values in a range fall into specified numeric intervals.

To Determine
a Frequency Distribution of Cell Values:

1. Bring up the Main Menu and select **Data**.

2. Select **Distribution** from the second-level menu.

3. Answer the "Enter values range" prompt by defining a range comprising a series of numeric values you want to analyze.

4. Press ⏎ or click the mouse.

5. Answer the "Enter bin range" prompt by defining a range containing the numeric grouping values, or bins, to use in the analysis.

6. Press ⏎ or click the mouse to complete the operation.

● **NOTES**   Cells in the values range that are blank or contain labels are ignored in a data-distribution analysis.

Numeric values found in the bin range represent the top value used for each individual bin. An entry from the values range is counted for a particular bin if its value exceeds the preceding bin range value—the one in the row above—and does not exceed the current bin's value.

Be careful when you use this command, because the number of cells from the values range that fall into particular bins are placed in the cells adjacent and to the right of the bin value, and anything in those cells is overwritten. The number of values that exceed the largest bin value is placed in this right-side column but one row below the largest bin value.

Examples

Suppose that your worksheet contains a variable number of student names, say 25 to 200, and grades and you want to know the number of students who have A, B, C, D, and F grade averages. You've used /**Range Name Create** to assign GRADES as the name of the cell range that contains the numeric grades, and you've entered the following five numbers in the cell range E3..E7, each of which is to be a bin range: 59, 69, 79, 89, and 100.

Select /**Data Distribution**. When 1-2-3 prompts you for the values range, press **F3** to switch to Names mode. Select GRADES for the values range. When 1-2-3 prompts you for the bin range, specify E3..E7. The distribution results are written into cells F3..F8, and they tell you how many value entries in GRADES fell into the five bins (0–59, 60–69, 70–79, 80–89, 90–100) representing grades F, D, C,

B, and A. In this example, the sixth bin for numbers greater than 100 is probably going to be zero, unless there was an error in the values range or extra credit was given for certain scores.

See Also   /Data Fill.

THE /DATA
FILL COMMAND

● **PURPOSE**   To initialize a cell range to a series of uniformly distributed values.

To Fill a Series
of Cells with Equally Spaced Values:

1. Bring up the Main Menu and select **Data**.

2. Select **Fill** from the second-level menu.

3. Answer the "Enter fill range" prompt by defining the range to receive the automatically generated values.

4. Press ↵ or click the mouse.

5. Answer the "Start" prompt by typing in the value for the first cell in the range.

6. Answer the "Step" prompt by typing in the separation value between each cell in the range.

7. Answer the "Stop" prompt in line three by typing in the value for the last cell in the range.

8. Press ↵ or click the mouse to complete the operation.

● **NOTES**   The default Stop value is 8191. Any value for Stop that exceeds the desired final number in the range works equally well. If your Stop value is smaller than the resulting sequence requires, the number of generated values will not fill the range. Each succeeding value is generated by adding the Step value to the preceding cell's value. The first value in the range is always the Start value. Each succeeding value is generated by adding the Step value, and 1-2-3 makes sure that the Stop value is never exceeded.

Examples

Suppose that you are preparing a worksheet of amortization values for a mortgage payment schedule. A thirty-year mortgage will require 360, one for each month's information. **/Data Fill** can automatically generate the month numbers for you.

Select **/Data Fill**. Answer the "Enter fill range" prompt by specifying cells A1..A360. Type a Start value of **1**, a Step value of **1**, and leave the Stop value at its default value of **8191**. When you complete the command, 1-2-3 fills in each of the first 360 cells of column A with numeric values (representing months) from 1 to 360.

See Also   /Data Distribution, /Data Sort, and /Data Table.

THE /DATA MATRIX COMMAND

● **PURPOSE**   To perform common matrix minipulations.

To Invert a Matrix:

1.   Bring up the Main Menu and select **Data**.

2.   Select **Matrix** from the second-level menu.

3.   Select **Invert** from the third-level menu.

4. Answer the "Enter range to invert" prompt by defining the range that contains the square matrix of values to be inverted.

5. Answer the "Enter output range" prompt by defining the range, or top-left corner of the range, where 1-2-3 will write the inverted matrix.

6. Press ↵ or click the mouse.

To Matrix-Multiply One Cell Range by Another:

1. Bring up the Main Menu and select **Data**.

2. Select **Matrix** from the second-level menu.

3. Select **Multiply** from the third-level menu.

4. Answer the "Enter first range to multiply" prompt by defining the range that contains one matrix of values to be multiplied.

5. Answer the "Enter second range to multiply" prompt by defining the range that contains the second matrix of values to be multiplied by the first.

6. Answer the "Enter output range" prompt by defining the range, or top-left corner of the range, that is to receive the results of the matrix multiplication.

7. Press ↵ or click the mouse to complete the operation.

● **NOTES**   You may only invert a square matrix, and it can't be larger than 90 cells square. Not all square matrices can even be inverted because there is no solution to the related equations.

When you multiply two matrices, the number of columns in the first matrix must equal the number of rows in the second matrix.

Examples

Suppose that you must solve the following set of simultaneous linear equations:

$$2x + 5y + 2z = 1$$
$$5x + 2y + 3z = 2$$
$$3x - 3y + 5z = -4$$

To do so, you must use both matrix manipulation commands. First, set up a 3 × 3 matrix of coefficients. As Figure II.1 shows, this original matrix appears in range A1..C3. By selecting **/Data Matrix Invert**, you can identify this range as the one to invert, and respond with cell A12 as the output range. The inverted matrix will be written into range A12..C14.

To complete the solution of the simultaneous linear equations, issue the **/Data Matrix Multiply** command to multiply this inverted matrix by the values found in the one-dimensional matrix in cells

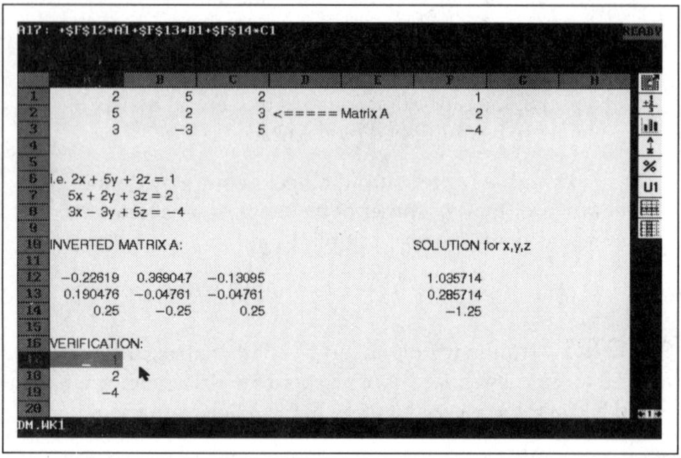

Figure II.1: Using matrix techniques for linear algebra

F1..F3. Specifying these two matrices as the first and second ones to multiply will produce solutions for x, y, and z in the output range F12..F14. For those of you familiar with linear algebra, a trio of verification formula appear in cells A17..A19. You can see the first of the three formulas at the top of Figure II.1.

THE /DATA PARSE COMMAND

• **PURPOSE**   To divide a wide column of non-delimited text labels into separate columns of cell data.

To Initiate the /Data Parse Command:

1.   Bring up the Main Menu and select **Data**.

2.   Select **Parse** from the second-level menu. A third-level menu, shown below, appears. You must select and complete each of the first three choices on the menu before parsing can be completed.

Format-Line Input-Column Output-Range Reset
Go Quit

3.   After you've selected and completed the first three choices on this menu, select **Go** to have 1-2-3 perform the actual parsing operation.

The first three choices—**Format-Line**, **Input Column**, and **Output-Range**—are explained in the sections below. To clear the current values for the input column and output range, you can select **Reset**. When you wish to exit from the /Data Parse command completely, select **Quit**. This returns you to Ready mode.

To Create a Format Line for Parsing:

1. Move the cell pointer to the first, or topmost, cell in the column of long labels to be divided.

2. Select **/Data Parse** and choose **Format-Line Create**. This tells 1-2-3 to define a line of symbols indicating how the long labels are to be divided. Each group of characters is known as a block.

3. Press ↵ or click the mouse to complete the operation.

The format line is inserted in your worksheet. No information is lost from the line above your long labels.

To Edit a Format Line before Parsing:

1. Move the cell pointer to a cell that contains an existing format line.

2. Select **/Data Parse** and choose **Format-Line Edit**. 1-2-3 will adjust its automatic encodings to suit the data in your long labels.

3. Press → and ← to position the cursor at the beginning character position of a block, and type any of the following symbols in the format line:

D   Begins a Date

L   Begins a Label

S   Skips a block

T   Begins a Time

V   Begins a Value

>   Fills in character positions

*   Enters a blank space

4. Press ↵ or click the mouse to complete the operation and return to the Data Parse Main Menu.

To Identify a Single
Column of Labels to Parse:

1. After you've selected **/Data Parse**, choose **Input-Column**.

2. Move the cell pointer to the format line that heads the column of long labels you want to parse.

3. Anchor the cell pointer and extend the highlight down the column to span all the labels you want parsed.

4. Press ↵ or click the mouse to complete the operation and return to the Data Parse Main Menu.

When you specify a column of labels to use as the input range, be sure to begin your range with the format line itself, not the first data-entry you want parsed.

To Identify
the Destination Range for Parsed Data:

1. Select **/Data Parse** and choose **Output-Range**.

2. Move the cell pointer to the blank area of the worksheet that will receive the data after it has been parsed.

3. Press ↵ or click the mouse to complete the operation and return to the Data Parse Main Menu.

● **NOTES** Use this Data Parse command to divide a single column of long labels into a number of distinct columnar entries. Usually, this is necessary after you've imported a non-delimited set of lines or records into 1-2-3 from a database management or word processing program.

First create a format line with the **/Data Parse Format-Line** command just above the column of long labels you want to be divided. Next, identify the Input-Column with the long labels (and format line). Finally, specify the Output-Range to receive the divided data. Only after these preparatory steps are completed can you select **/Data Parse Go** to actually separate the data.

Examples

Suppose you've imported a column of long labels from a database management program, and the labels contain an employee ID, lastname, firstname, and phone column, like so:

733 Robbins	Judd	(415)566-3984
923 Carlson	Samuel	(415)222-2938
193 Bingham	Joan	(408)335-5998

If these sample labels appear in cells A2, A3, and A4, you can divide this single column of labels into four separate columns. First, create a format line by moving the cell pointer to A2 and choosing **Format-Line Create** on the **/Data Parse** menu. Next, identify the combination format line and data by choosing **Input-Column** and defining the range as A2..A5. Finally, define the **Output-Range** as A15. When you choose **Go**, 1-2-3 will divide your long labels, beginning in row 15, into values written into column A, and labels written into columns B, C, and D.

See Also /File Import.

THE /DATA
QUERY COMMAND

● **PURPOSE** To search through, select, or extract information from a 1-2-3 database.

To Initiate the /Data Query Command:

1. Bring up the Main Menu and select **Data**.

2. Select **Query** from the second-level menu that appears. A third-level menu appears with the following choices, the

first seven of which are explained in the subsequent sections below:

Input   Criteria   Output   Find   Extract   Unique   Delete
Reset   Quit

3.   Select one choice according to the action you now wish to perform.

To clear the current values for the input, criteria, and output ranges, you can select **Reset**. When you wish to exit from the /Data Query command completely, select **Quit**. You will return to Ready mode.

To Identify the Data Records to Be Searched:

1.   Select **Input** from the /Data Query menu.

2.   Answer the "Enter input range" prompt by specifying a range of cells that spans both the row of column labels heading your data and the data itself.

3.   Press ↵ or click the mouse to return to the /Data Query Main Menu.

The **Input** command identifies the database, or portion of one, you want searched with the Extract, Delete, Find, and Unique operations. The Input range must include your data rows *and* a row of field names located just above the data.

To Specify the Searching Criteria to Use:

1.   Select **Criteria** from the /Data Query menu.

2.   Answer the "Enter criteria range" prompt by specifying a range of cells that spans both the desired field names and the record selection conditions.

3.   Press ↵ or click the mouse to return to the /Data Query Main Menu.

You can include all or only some of the field names from the original database table in the first row of your criteria range. Only data columns for which you've included field names in the criteria range can be treated by the conditional tests contained in the remaining criteria range.

Remaining rows in your criteria range contain selection conditions. These conditions can be exact matches or they can be looser relational expressions to be satisfied. All conditions that appear on the same row are logically treated as if connected by AND operators. Each group of conditions that appears on a separate row is logically treated as if connected to other condition rows by OR operators.

To Indicate Where
Output Records Are to Be Placed:

1. Select **Output** from the /Data Query menu.

2. Answer the "Enter output range" prompt by specifying the range of cells that spans the desired field names.

3. Press ↵ or click the mouse to return to the /Data Query Main Menu.

Use the **/Copy** command to ensure that the specified field names in the Output range are exact matches of the original database's field names. Be careful, because if your output range is a single row with field names only, 1-2-3 will erase all information below those specified output field names. Look below to ensure that no important data will be erased.

To keep the output to a fixed number of rows, you can define an output range to include a specific group of rows (larger than one). 1-2-3 will only write as many output records as it can fit into that range.

To Highlight Records
Successively that Match the Criteria:

1. After you've prepared the Input and Criteria ranges, select **Find** from the /Data Query menu.

2. 1-2-3 highlights the first row in the database table that meets the specified criteria. Use the following keystrokes to view of the records that meet the criteria:

↑	Moves to the next matching record.
↓	Moves to the previous matching record.
→	Moves to the next field in the record.
←	Moves to the previous field in the record.
F2	Allows you to edit the current field.
Home	Highlights the first record in the input range.
End	Highlights the last record in the input range.

3. Press ↵ or click the mouse to return to the /Data Query Main Menu.

To Make a Copy
of All Records that Match the Criteria:

1. Define the Input, Criteria, and Output ranges with the appropriate choices on the /Data Query menu.

2. Select **Extract** from the /Data Query Main Menu. The copying, or extraction, is performed immediately and control returns to the /Data Query Main Menu.

To Eliminate Duplicate
Records during an Extraction:

1. Define the Input, Criteria, and Output ranges with appropriate choices from the /Data Query menu.

2. Select **Unique** from the /Data Query Main Menu. The copying, or extraction, is performed immediately and control returns to the /Data Query Main Menu.

Remember that you can extract some or all fields from the records that meet certain criteria. After the extraction, and before writing the matching records into the output range, 1-2-3 looks for duplications in the output records. It is quite conceivable that certain original database table records have some equivalent fields and differ in others. If only the equivalent field names are listed in the output range, these duplicated records will not appear in the output range when you choose **Unique**; however, they will appear if you choose **Extract**.

To Delete Records that Match the Criteria:

1. Define the Input, Criteria, and Output ranges with appropriate choices from the /Data Query menu.

2. Select **Delete** from the /Data Query Main Menu.

3. If you're sure you want to remove all records matching the criteria from the input range, select **Delete** from the new submenu that appears. Otherwise, select **Cancel**. After either choice, control returns to the /Data Query Main Menu.

Examples

In Figure II.2, a sample database of three records appears at the top of the screen (the Input range is A1..D4). A criteria range is set up in the middle of the screen in cells A8..D9, and an output range is set up to begin with the specified field names seen in A15..D15.

Suppose your company writes birthday bonus checks, and you want to extract all records for employees born in February. Bring up the **/Data Query** menu and successively select Input, Criteria, and Output to specify the appropriate ranges. Next, select **Extract**.

See Also "The Basics of Database Management" in Part I.

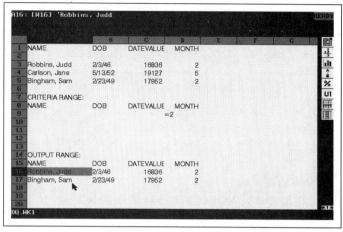

Figure II.2: Extracting records with the /Data Query command

THE /DATA REGRESSION COMMAND

- **PURPOSE**   To predict future values based on current values, using a conventional regression analysis.

To Initiate the /Data Regression Command:

1.   Bring up the Main Menu and select **Data**.

2.   Select **Regression** from the second-level menu. A third-level menu appears from which you must select and complete at least the first three choices:

X-Range Y-Range Output-Range Intercept Reset Go
Quit

3.   Select one choice according to the action you wish to perform.

4. Select **Go** to tell 1-2-3 to perform the actual regression operation.

The first three choices—**X-Range**, **Y-Range**, **Output Range**—are explained in the subsequent sections here. 1-2-3 automatically computes a y-axis intercept by default, but you can select **Intercept** to set the y-axis intercept to zero. When you select **Reset**, 1-2-3 clears the current values for the X, Y, and Output ranges, and also restores the Intercept setting to Compute. To exit from the /Data Regression command completely, select **Quit**. You will return to Ready mode.

To Identify the Independent Variables for the X-Range:

1. Select **X-Range** from the /Data Regression menu.

2. Answer the "Enter independent variables, or X-range" prompt by specifying the columnar range of cells that spans the one or more independent variables.

3. Press ↵ or click the mouse to return to the /Data Regression Main Menu.

You can perform multiple linear regression analysis by specifying from two to sixteen columns of independent variable values. However, you must be sure to include the same number of rows in the X-ranges as exist in the single column—and dependent—Y-range.

To Identify the Dependent Variables for the Y-Range:

1. Select **Y-Range** from the /Data Regression menu.

2. Answer the "Enter dependent variable, or Y-range" prompt by specifying a columnar range of cells that contains the dependent (or Y) variable.

3. Press ↵ or click the mouse to return to the /Data Regression Main Menu.

To Identify Where to Place the Regression Results:

1. Select **Output-Range** from the /Data Regression menu.

2. Answer the "Enter output range" prompt by moving the cell pointer to the top-left corner of a blank range. All output calculations will be written to this area of the worksheet.

3. Press ↵ or click the mouse to return to the /Data Regression Main Menu.

● **NOTES**   The output range receives several values from a /Data Regression analysis. Table II.1 briefly explains the meaning of each of these values.

Examples

Suppose you were analyzing long distance leased line costs for a new business. Based on your recent bills, you wish to budget for phone expenses over the coming months, and you plan to use 1-2-3's **/Data Regression** command. Over the last five months,

Table II.1: Data Regression Output Values

Constant	Y-Axis Intercept
Std Err of Y Est	Standard error between actual Y values (dependent variables) and those predicted by the regression line
R Squared	Indicator of the regression line's reliability (from 0 to 1, with 1 being most reliable)
No. of Observations	Count of the number of rows in the X and Y ranges
Degrees of Freedom	Number of independent variable values minus the number of independent variables minus one
X Coefficient(s)	Slope of the regression line
Std Err of Coef.	Standard error of the X coefficient(s)

you've had five telephone bills of $225, $350, $600, $1100, and $1600. You place these five numbers into the cell range E6..E10. Meanwhile, in cell range D6..D10, you place the number of calls made in the five months—250, 500, 1000, 2000, and 3000.

After initiating the **/Data Regression** command, you choose **X-Range** and specify D6..D10 as the value of the independent variable. Next, you choose **Y-Range** and specify E6..E10 as the value of the dependent variable. Seeing that your worksheet is blank below row ten, you choose **Output-Range** and specify A12. To complete the regression analysis, you select **Go,** which produces all the analytical results in rows 12 through 20. This particular set of numbers produces a constant of 100 and an X coefficient of 0.5, representing the equation $Y = 100 + (0.5 * X)$. Future phone expenses can be calculated by adding the flat fixed fee of $100 to a variable fee based on 50 cents per call.

THE /DATA SORT COMMAND

- **PURPOSE** To alphabetize or numerically order the information in any range of cells.

To Initiate the /Data Sort Command:

1. Bring up the Main Menu and select **Data**.

2. Select **Sort** from the second-level menu. A third-level menu appears from which you must select and complete at least the first three choices:

Data-Range Primary-Key Secondary-Key Reset
Go Quit

3. Select one choice according to the action you wish to perform.

4. Select **Go** to tell 1-2-3 to perform the sorting operation.

The first two choices—**Primary-key** and **Data-Range**—are explained in the sections below. Select **Secondary-Key** to tell 1-2-3 how to arrange records which have the same value for their primary keys. To clear the current values for the data range and the sorting key or keys, select **Reset**. When you wish to exit from the /Data Sort command completely, select **Quit**. You will return to 1-2-3 Ready mode.

To Specify a Group of Cells (the Records) to Arrange:

1. Select /**Data Sort** and **Data-Range**.

2. Answer the "Enter data range" prompt by specifying the range of cells that contains the data records. Do not include the field names row in this range.

3. Press ↵ or click the mouse to return to the /Data Sort Main Menu.

To Tell 1-2-3 How to Arrange the Specified Records:

1. After you've selected /**Data Sort**, choose **Primary-Key**.

2. Answer the "Primary sort key" prompt by moving the cell pointer to any cell in the column that contains the field of data on which to arrange all the rows of the database table.

3. Answer the "Sort order (A or D)" prompt by typing **A** for an ascending sort, or **D** for a descending sort.

4. Press ↵ or click the mouse to return to the /Data Sort Main Menu.

Ascending sorts arrange labels from A to Z and numbers in increasing numeric order. If a field contains both labels and values, labels are arranged first, and remaining values next.

Examples

Suppose your employee records database table extends from A3 through G60, the field names appear in row three, and column B contains employee last names. You want to arrange and then print all employee records in alphabetical order by name.

Bring up the **/Data Sort** menu and choose **Data-Range**. Define the range as A4..G60, which spans the employee records but not the field name row. Choose **Primary-Key**, move the cell pointer to any cell in column B and press ↵ or click the mouse. Type **A** for an ascending sort to complete the sorting preparatory steps. Finally, choose **Go** to direct 1-2-3 to start rearranging the data records on the worksheet.

See Also   /Data Fill.

THE /DATA
TABLE COMMAND

● **PURPOSE**   To create a table of resulting formula values, based on the effects of changing one or more variables.

To Initiate the /Data Table Command:

1.   Bring up the Main Menu and select **Data**.

2.   Select **Table** from the second-level menu. A third-level menu appears with the following choices:

   1 2 Reset

3.   Select one choice according to the action you wish to perform.

The first two choices are explained in the subsequent sections below. To clear the current values for the table ranges and the input cells, select **Reset**. This returns you to Ready mode.

To Change One
Variable in One or More Formulas:

1.   Select one cell in your worksheet to represent the variable in a formula, and enter a sample number in that cell.

2.   Select an open portion of your worksheet for the data table. Be sure to leave the top-left corner of this table range blank.

3.   Enter a series of possible values for the variable in the first column of cells, starting with the second row of the table range.

4.   Enter a one-variable formula in the top cell of the table's second column.

5.   Select /**Data Table** and choose **1**.

6.   Answer the "Enter table range" prompt by specifying a complete range of cells to span the entire table.

7.   Answer the "Enter input cell 1" prompt by specifying the variable's representative cell that you selected in step 1 above.

8.   Press ↵ or click the mouse to return to Ready mode. All table entries are calculated and entered automatically.

● **NOTES**   In a Data Table 1, the complete table range must include a leftmost column of variable values, with the top-left cell above these values left blank. The top cell in the second column of the table must contain a formula that uses the variables from the first column to produce the resulting values in the remaining cells of the table.

To Change Two Variables in One Formula:

1.   Select one cell in your worksheet to represent one variable in a formula that uses two variables, and enter a sample number in that cell.

2. Select a second cell in your worksheet to represent the second variable in the same formula, and enter a sample number in that cell as well.

3. Select an open portion of your worksheet for the entire data table. Enter the basic two-variable formula in the top-left corner cell of this area. Refer to the two cells specified in steps 1 and 2.

4. Enter a series of possible values for the first variable in the column of cells immediately below the formula.

5. Enter a series of possible values for the second variable in the row of cells immediately to the right of the formula.

6. Select /**Data Table** and choose **2**.

7. Answer the "Enter table range" prompt by specifying a complete range of cells that spans the entire table.

8. Answer the "Enter input cell 1" prompt by specifying the first variable's representative cell that you selected in step 1 above.

9. Answer the "Enter input cell 2" prompt by specifying the second variable's representative cell that you selected in step 2 above.

10. Press ↵ or click the mouse to return to Ready mode.

● **NOTES** In a Data Table 2, the complete table range must include a leftmost column of variable values, and a top row with a second set of variable values. The top-left corner cell of the table must include a formula that uses both variables to produce the resulting values in the remaining cells of the table.

Examples

Suppose you ran a limousine service and you wanted to produce a chart for your drivers listing their vehicles' mileage per gallon (MPG). You could define cell D5 to represent the first variable, miles driven, for a Data Table 2 example, and define cell D6 to represent the second variable, gallons of gas consumed. You could place the MPG formula (+D5/D6) in cell D12, and place four

sample values for miles driven in cells E12..H12: 1000, 2000, 3000,
4000. In cells D13..D20, you could enter eight sample values for gallons consumed. By bringing up the **/Data Table** menu, selecting **2**,
entering D12..H20 as the data table range, D5 as input cell 1 (for the
column values), and D6 as input cell 2 (for the row values), you
would have your list. All table values are automatically calculated
and entered for you.

See Also   /Data Fill

THE /FILE ADMIN COMMAND

● **PURPOSE**   To perform housekeeping chores for disk files.

To Initiate the /File Admin Command:

1. Bring up the Main Menu and select **File**.

2. Select **Admin** from the second-level menu. A third-level
menu appears with the following choices:

Reservation   Table   Link-Refresh

3. Select one choice according to the action you wish to
perform.

The first two choices are explained in the sections below. To update
the values in cells that are linked to disk-based worksheets by formulas, select **Link-Refresh**. This returns you to Ready mode.

To Obtain or Release a File Reservation:

1. Select **/File Admin** and choose **Reservation**.

2.   A third-level menu appears, with two choices: **Get** and **Release**.

   a.   To secure the file's reservation, and be able to save a changed version of it, select **Get**.

   b.   To release a reservation that you currently hold, and let others make changes and save them, select **Release**.

This command can only be used meaningfully if the file is shared on a network. You reserve a file automatically when you issue the **/File Retrieve** command, unless someone else already has the reservation. In that case, 1-2-3 retrieves the file for you but places an RO, or read-only, indicator on the status line.

You must have reserved a shared file before 1-2-3 will allow you to save a changed version of it under the same name. You cannot make and save changes in this case, until and unless you get the reservation later.

To Create a Table of Information about a Group of Disk Files:

1.   Select **/File Admin** and choose **Table**.

2.   A third-level menu appears with five choices:

   Worksheet—Obtains the names of all worksheet files— .WK1, .WK3, or .WKS.

   Print—Obtains the names of all .PRN files.

   Graph—Obtains the names of all .PIC files.

   Other—Obtains the names of all files in a specified directory.

   Linked—Obtains the names of all files referenced in the current worksheet by linking formulas.

3.   Answer the "Enter directory" prompt by typing the name of the directory about which you want information; otherwise, press ↵ for data about the current directory. The "Enter directory" prompt does not appear if you select Linked in step 2.

4.   Answer the "Enter range for table" prompt by moving the cell pointer to a cell at the top-left corner of a blank four-column area of the worksheet and pressing ↵ or click the mouse. 1-2-3 writes information about the requested file types into this area of your worksheet.

Be careful, because 1-2-3 writes over any information in the area it needs to write table information—the name, date, time, and size of each file. The Table of Information requires four columns and as many rows plus one as there are files that meet the selected criteria type or types.

Examples

Save any file you are working on and select **/Worksheet Erase Yes** to clear the current worksheet. Next, select **/File Admin Table Worksheet** to request information about all worksheet files. When prompted for the directory, accept the default directory by pressing ↵. When 1-2-3 prompts you for the resulting table range, press ↵ to accept A1 as the location to begin writing the file information.

Columns A through D receive name, date, time, and size information for all files that meet the specification. You have to widen column 1 to see the full name of all files, and you have to use **/Range Format Date** to convert the date and time values in columns B and C into readable form.

See Also   /File List, /Range Trans, and /Range Value.

THE /FILE
COMBINE COMMAND

● **PURPOSE**   To adjust the current worksheet's values with values found in a disk-based worksheet.

To Initiate the /File Combine Command:

1. Move the cell pointer where you want 1-2-3 to begin incor-
porating data from a different file located on disk.

2. Bring up the Main Menu and select **File**.

3. Select **Combine** from the second-level menu.

4. A third-level menu, shown below, appears.

Copy—Replicates data from a disk file.

Add—Adds data numerically from a disk file.

Subtract—Subtracts data numerically from a disk file.

Select one command according to your needs.

To Copy Information from a Disk Worksheet into the Current Worksheet:

1. Select **/File Combine** and choose **Copy**.

2. Select either

- **Entire-File**, which copies an entire disk file into the current file; or

- **Named/Specified-Range**, which copies a portion of a
disk file. If you select this command, 1-2-3 will prompt
you to "Enter range name or address." Type the cell
range from the disk file that contains the data you want
to replicate in the current worksheet.

Regardless of which choice you make, the specified data is
written into the current worksheet beginning at the location of the cell pointer.

3. 1-2-3 switches to Files mode. Answer the "Enter name of
file to combine" prompt by selecting one of the names
from the list of files shown or by entering another name.
1-2-3 will switch to Wait mode while it copies the data
from the disk worksheet you just named.

To Use Values in a Disk Worksheet to Add to or Subtract from Current Worksheet Values:

1. Select **/File Combine** and choose either

- **Add**, which adds values from a disk-based worksheet to corresponding values in the current worksheet; or

- **Subtract**, which subtracts values in a disk-based worksheet from corresponding values in the current worksheet.

2. Select either

- **Entire-File**, which uses all values in the specified disk file; or

- **Named/Specified-Range**, which uses only a portion of the disk file. If you select **Named/Specified-Range**, 1-2-3 prompts you to "Enter range name or address." Type the desired cell range from the disk file that contains the data you want to use to adjust values in the current worksheet.

   Regardless of which choice you make, the data values are added to or subtracted from values in the current work-sheet. This operation only affects the current cell and other cells located to the right of and below it.

3. 1-2-3 switches to Files mode. Answer the "Enter name of file to combine" prompt by selecting one of the names from the list of files shown or by entering another name. 1-2-3 will switch to Wait mode while it reads values from the disk worksheet you just named and will perform the previously indicated addition or subtraction.

Examples

Suppose you have a useful macro in cells J3..N14 of your MONEYMKT worksheet, located on disk, and you'd like to use it in your CHECKING worksheet as well. Use **/File Retrieve** to make CHECKING the current worksheet, move the cell pointer to a blank portion of the worksheet, and select **/File Combine Copy Named/Specified-Range**. Type J3..N14 for the range address, and select

MONEYMKT.WK1 from the FILES list that appears. The macro will be written into CHECKING beginning at the location of the cell pointer. Remember that you must use **/Range Name Create** before you can actually run the macro code in the new worksheet.

See Also /Copy and /File Save.

THE /FILE
DIRECTORY COMMAND

● **PURPOSE** To specify a default file directory for the current work session only.

To Temporarily Change the Default Directory:

1. Bring up the Main Menu and select **File**.

2. Select **Directory** from the second-level menu.

3. Answer the "Enter current directory" prompt by typing the full path name of any disk directory.

4. Press ↵ or click the mouse to complete the operation.

● **NOTES** The directory you enter with this command becomes the default for the remainder of the current session only. If you want to change 1-2-3's default directory permanently, use the **/Worksheet Global Default Directory** and **/Worksheet Global Default Update** commands.

Examples

Suppose you intend to spend the entire day working with a variety of checking and finance worksheets. Rather than specifying a different directory each time you retrieve a new file, you could select **/File Directory**, and when 1-2-3 prompts you to type the name of the directory that stores the financial worksheets, you could type

D:\123\FINANCE. 1-2-3 will display a default list of worksheets from this directory for the remainder of the work session.

See Also /Worksheet Global.

THE /FILE ERASE COMMAND

● **PURPOSE** To permanently remove a disk file.

To Choose a File to Erase:

1. Bring up the Main Menu and select **File.**

2. Select **Erase** from the second-level menu.

3. A third-level menu appears with four choices:

Worksheet—Displays .WK? file names.

Print—Displays only .PRN file names.

Graph—Displays only .PIC file names.

Other—Displays all file names.

Select one choice to see a list of appropriate files from which to select.

4. 1-2-3 switches to Files mode. Answer the "Enter name of file to erase" prompt by selecting one of the names from the list of files shown or by entering another name. 1-2-3 will display a confirmation menu. Select **No** to withdraw your request to erase the file, or **Yes** to confirm your request and direct 1-2-3 to permanently erase the file from the disk.

● **NOTES** This command permanently removes a disk file. To erase only a portion of your worksheet, use /Range Erase. To erase one or more columns or rows, use /Worksheet Delete. To erase only the memory copy of a worksheet, use /Worksheet Erase.

Examples

To delete a 1990 budget worksheet called BUDGET90.WK1, select **/File Erase Worksheet**. In Files mode, select BUDGET90.WK1 and answer **Yes** to the confirmation prompt.

See Also /Range Erase, /Worksheet Delete, and /Worksheet Erase.

THE /FILE
IMPORT COMMAND

● **PURPOSE** To copy ASCII data from a disk file into the current worksheet.

To Read Non-Delimited
Text into a Single Column of Cells:

1. Move the cell pointer to the cell to which you'd like 1-2-3 to write the text lines located in a disk file.

2. Bring up the Main Menu and select **File**.

3. Select **Import** from the second-level menu.

4. Select **Text** to import successive lines of text into successive cells in the current column.

5. Answer the "Enter name of file to import" prompt by selecting a file name from the list of displayed .PRN (text) files. Or, if the list doesn't have the file whose text you want, type in a different file name.

1-2-3 reads all text lines from the file you specified into the column of your worksheet where the cell pointer is. Each line of text from the disk file, up to a maximum of 240 characters, is stored in a single long label in the current worksheet.

To Read Delimited Data into Separate Cells:

1.   Move the cell pointer to the cell to which you'd like 1-2-3 to write the text lines found in a disk file.

2.   Bring up the Main Menu and select **File**.

3.   Select **Import** from the second-level menu.

4.   Select **Numbers** to import the delimited fields from successive lines of text. They will be written into separate columns on successive rows of your worksheet.

5.   Answer the "Enter name of file to import" prompt by selecting one file name from the list of displayed .PRN (text) files. Or, if the list doesn't contain the file whose text you want, type in a different file name.

• NOTES   To import both labels and numbers into separate columns of a worksheet, the data must reside in a delimited text file on disk. This means that all fields are separated from one another with delimiting symbols, such as quotation marks around labels or commas. If you attempt to import a non-delimited file with the Numbers choice, 1-2-3 will ignore all label-type data. If you only have access to a nondelimited file, use the Text choice and the /Data Parse command to separate the column of data into individual fields.

Examples

Suppose your personal finances program generates a series of expense and income forms, and each form can be printed or stored in a non-delimited text file. However, you want to perform some additional analysis on your expenses. You create a EXPENSES.TXT file with your finances program, bring up 1-2-3 and, from the blank initial worksheet screen, select **/File Import Text**. After you type in the complete directory path name to EXPENSES.TXT, all the textual information is read into column A. But you want to separate this non-delimited data, so you use the **/Data Parse** command to separate the numeric information into distinct columns. Finally, you adjust the formatting and column widths before you continue with your 1-2-3 analyses.

See Also /Data Parse, /Print File, and the @TRIM and @VALUE functions.

THE /FILE LIST COMMAND

• **PURPOSE** To display date, time, and size information about disk files.

To Display All File Names of a Specified Type:

1. Bring up the Main Menu and select **File**.

2. Select **List** from the second-level menu.

3. A third-level menu appears with five choices:

Worksheet—Obtains the names of all .WK1, .WK3, or .WKS worksheet files.

Print—Obtains the names of all .PRN files.

Graph—Obtains the names of all .PIC files.

Other—Obtains the names of all files in a specified directory.

Linked—Obtains the names of all files referenced in the current worksheet by linking formulas.

Select one of these choices.

4. 1-2-3 temporarily displays a screen with the file names of the type you specified. To highlight a file name, press the cursor movement keys or press and hold down button one of the mouse and move the mouse pointer around the screen. As each file name is highlighted, its date and time of last modification, as well as its file size, appear at the top of the screen.

5. Press ↵ or release mouse button one to return to Ready mode and restore your worksheet screen to its former status.

● **NOTES** The file name display is temporary and does not affect any worksheet activity or contents. Use /File Admin Table to create a more permanent list of file information.

See Also /File Admin.

THE /FILE RETRIEVE COMMAND

● **PURPOSE** To load a worksheet file into memory.

To Select a Worksheet on Disk to Load into Memory:

1. Bring up the Main Menu and select **File**.

2. Select **Retrieve** from the second-level menu. If you haven't saved the current worksheet changes, a simple but protective confirmation menu will appear. Choose **Yes** to confirm or **No** to withdraw the retrieval request.

   a. If you choose **Yes** in step 2, 1-2-3 switches to Files mode. Answer the "Name of file to retrieve" prompt by selecting one of the names from the list of files shown, or by typing another name.

● **NOTES** If you have not saved your current work when you select /File Retrieve, 1-2-3 will beep and remind you that worksheet changes have not been saved. You can withdraw the retrieval request and issue the /File Save command to back up your work before continuing. Alternatively, you can discard your current work by allowing the specified file to be retrieved and written over your current work.

See Also   /File Admin and /File Directory.

THE /FILE
SAVE COMMAND

● **PURPOSE**   To save a copy of your memory worksheet information into a disk file.

To Back Up
the Current Worksheet in a Disk File:

1. Bring up the Main Menu and select **File**.

2. Select **Save** from the second-level menu.

3. Answer the "Enter name of file to save" prompt by typing
   a name in which to store the current worksheet, or by
   pressing ↵ to accept the name that is already displayed
   (this is the name under which you retrieved or saved the
   file previously).

   At this point you can password-protect the file by pressing
   a space and typing **P** before typing the file name or pressing ↵ in step 3. The program will ask you to enter a
   password—it can be up to 15 characters long and won't
   display on the screen. You'll be asked to enter it twice so
   you don't make a typographical error.

4. If the name selected already exists on disk, a new menu appears containing three choices:

   ● **Cancel** does not overwrite the existing disk file.

- **Replace** proceeds with overwriting the disk file with a copy of the current worksheet.
- **Backup** saves the disk file with a .BAK extension and the current worksheet with a specified name and the .WK1 extension.

Examples

Suppose you are working on a new worksheet and after an hour you select **/File Save** to back up your work. 1-2-3 informs you that another worksheet of that same name exists already. You select **Cancel** to avoid overwriting someone else's work, and you choose **/File Save** again, this time entering a completely different name.

See Also /File Combine, /File Directory, and /File Xtract.

THE /FILE XTRACT COMMAND

- **PURPOSE** To copy a portion of the current worksheet into a separate worksheet file on disk.

To Copy Formulas, Values, and Labels from Your Current Worksheet to a Disk Worksheet:

1. Bring up the Main Menu and select **File**.

2. Select **Xtract** from the second-level menu.

3. Select **Formulas** to store a complete copy of an existing range of cell contents and formulas into a new disk worksheet, or select **Values** to store only existing cell contents—that is, computed or calculated results—into a new worksheet.

4. Answer the "Enter name of file to extract to" prompt by typing a name in which to store the range of cells, or by selecting one of the names being displayed on line three.

5. Answer the "Enter extract range" prompt by highlighting the range of cells you want 1-2-3 to copy into a separate disk worksheet.

6. If the name selected already exists on disk, a new menu appears with three choices:

- **Cancel** ends the copy procedure and does not overwrite the existing disk file.

- **Replace** overwrites the disk file with a copy of the specified cell range.

- **Backup** saves disk file with a .BAK extension and writes the specified cell range to a worksheet with the specified name and .WK1 extension.

Select one choice.

• NOTES To write the most current values, remember to press F9 (CALC) to update your worksheet values prior to using /File Xtract Values command. Also, when extracting formulas, remember to define the range to include all cells referred to in all formulas that you are extracting.

Examples

Suppose your PAYROLL worksheet includes employee names and wage data, as well as the summary data, categorized by departmental codes. Employee salaries are classified, but you need to pass along the departmental summary numbers to your managers for further budgeting analysis. The employee salary information might occupy the first 10 columns of the worksheet, while a macro performs database manipulations and summations and stores the results in columns R to Z. Select **/File Xtract Values**, and specify SUMMARY as the new file name to receive just the summary cell range. Next, enter the appropriate extract range and press ↵ or click the mouse to complete the operation.

See Also /Copy.

THE /GRAPH A (OR B, C, D, E, F)COMMAND

● **PURPOSE**   To define the range or ranges of data to be graphed—that is, used as Y-axis values.

To Specify the First (through the Sixth) Data Range to Graph:

1.   Bring up the Main Menu and select **Graph**.

2.   Select **A** from the second-level menu.

3.   Answer the "Enter first data range" prompt by highlighting the range of cells to graph.

4.   Press ⏎ or click the mouse to complete the specification and return to the /Graph Main Menu.

● **NOTES**   To define a second to sixth range to graph, repeat these steps but choose B through F on the /Graph Main Menu.

Examples

Suppose you have a worksheet that performs a break-even analysis for your production business. In cells A6..B9, you have three entries and a total for fixed costs:

1. R&D	$35,000.00
2. Advertising	$100,000.00
3. Overhead	$20,000.00
TOTAL FIXED:	$155,000.00

Select /**Graph A** and specify the right-hand group of four numbers as the first data range (B6..B9) to graph. The /Graph Main Menu reappears and B6..B9 appears in the Ranges box of the Graph Settings display.

See Also   /Graph Group.

THE /GRAPH GROUP COMMAND

● **PURPOSE**   To specify all graphing ranges at the same time.

To Define All Data Ranges with One Operation:

1. Bring up the Main Menu and select **Graph**.

2. Select **Group** from the second-level menu.

3. Answer the "Enter group range" prompt by highlighting a range of cells that begins with the X range and continues with the A (and possibly B through F) range or ranges.

4. Select **Columnwise** or **Rowwise** to indicate whether the columns or rows of the range contain the groups of data values to graph.

5. Press ↵ or click the mouse to complete the specification of multiple ranges before returning to the /Graph Main Menu.

Examples

Suppose your break-even worksheet stores a sequence of values for Production Units Sold in cells F6..F14, the Revenues Produced by those units stored in cells G6..G14, and the Variable Costs incurred during production in cells H6..H14. To quickly define the X range (Production Units on the X axis) and the two Y ranges (Revenues for the A range, and Variable Costs for the B range), select **/Graph Group**. Specify F6..H14 as the group range, and specify **column-wise**. The Graph Settings window is instantaneously updated with these three ranges.

THE /GRAPH NAME COMMAND

• **PURPOSE**   To assign a name to each unique graph within a single worksheet, and to manage all named graphs within the worksheet.

To Initiate the /Graph Name Command:

1.   Bring up the Main Menu and select **Graph**.

2.   Select **Name** from the second-level menu. A third-level menu appears with the following choices:

Use   Create   Delete   Reset   Table

3.   Select one choice according to the action you wish to perform.

All choices but the **Reset** choice are explained in the sections below. Select **Reset** to delete all named graphs in the worksheet and return to the second-level /Graph menu.

To Name, Access,
or Delete a Worksheet Graph:

1. After choosing **/Graph Name**, select one of the following:

- **Use** to switch to a different named graph.
- **Create** to name the current graph.
- **Delete** to remove an entry for a current graph.

2. Type the desired or existing graph name.

To Display a List of All
Named Graphs in the Current Worksheet:

1. Choose **/Graph Name** and select **Table**.

2. Answer the "Enter range for table" prompt by moving the cell pointer to the top-left corner of a blank area where you want 1-2-3 to write the table of graphs that exist in your worksheet.

3. Press ⌐ or click the mouse to complete the operation.

A Graph Table requires three columns. 1-2-3 writes the name, graph type, and first line of the title into these columns. To do this, 1-2-3 requires as many rows as there are named graphs in your worksheet.

Examples

To assign the name REVENUES to the currently defined graph settings, select **/Graph Name Create** and enter REVENUES in response to the prompt. To restore the settings in a previously named graph called FIXED-COSTS, select **/Graph Name Use** and type FIXED-COSTS in response to the prompt. The formerly defined graph will appear on your monitor. Press **Esc** to clear the screen of the graph and restore the /Graph Main Menu. Select **Quit** to return to Ready mode.

See Also /File Save, /Graph Save, and /Graph View.

THE /GRAPH OPTIONS COMMAND

• **PURPOSE**   To customize a variety of aspects of individual graphs.

To Initiate the /Graph Options Command:

1.   Bring up the Main Menu and select **Graph**.

2.   Select **Options** from the second-level menu. A third-level menu appears with the following choices:

Legend Format Titles Grid Scale Color B&W Data-Labels Quit

3.   Select one choice according to the action you wish to perform.

The principal choices are explained in the sections below. To display the graph in color or monochrome, choose **Color** or **B&W**. Choosing **Quit** returns you to the previous /Graph menu.

To Assign Legends to Data Ranges:

1.   Select **/Graph Options** and choose **Legend**.

2.   A submenu appears that offers seven choices:

A B C D E F Range

Choose one of these, according to whether you will enter a data legend now or use existing worksheet labels.

• Select **A** to **F** to enter a text legend for one of the six possible data ranges. You can type the legend yourself or assign the contents of a cell by entering a backslash (\) and the cell identifier.

• Select **Range** to assign a pre-existing group of worksheet labels as the legends to use.

3.   Depending on your choice in step 2,

  • Answer the "Enter legend for first (or second through sixth) data range" prompt by typing in the text 1-2-3 should use.

  • Answer the "Enter legend range" prompt by highlighting the range of up to six adjacent labels that you want 1-2-3 to use as the text legends.

4.   Press ↵ or click the mouse to complete the operation.

To Enter Titles
for the Graph Itself and for the Two Axes:

1.   Select **/Graph Options** and choose **Titles**.

2.   A submenu appears that offers four titling choices:

   First—Enters the first line of the graph's title.

   Second—Enters the second line of the graph's title.

   X-Axis—Enters a title for the X-axis.

   Y-Axis—Enters a title for the Y-axis.

   Select the choice you are ready to specify.

3.   In response to 1-2-3's prompt for your selected title, type in the desired text and press ↵.

4.   Select **Quit** to return to the /Graph Main Menu.

To Specify X-Axis and Y-Axis Scaling:

1.   Select **/Graph Options** and choose **Scale**.

2.   A submenu appears with three scaling choices:

   Y-Scale—Sets scaling for the Y-axis.

   X-Scale—Sets scaling for the X-axis.

   Skip—Displays only every n'th value on the X-axis.

   Select the choice you want for your data.

If you selected **Y-Scale** or **X-Scale** in step 2, choose the type of scaling from the following submenu:

Automatic—Computes the scale based on the range of data values.

Manual—Uses specified maximum and minimum scale values.

Lower—Sets the minimum scale value.

Upper—Sets the maximum scale value.

Format—Sets the cell format for displayed axis values.

Indicator—Display or hides the scaling factor.

Display—Controls the location and display of Y-axis labels and tick marks.

Quit—Returns to the preceding menu.

Once you've chosen a scaling type, select **Quit** twice to return to the /Graph Main Menu.

If you selected Skip in step 2, type an *n* value to represent the skipping interval and select **Quit** to return to the /Graph Main Menu.

To Assign Labels to the Data Ranges:

1. Select **/Graph Options** and choose **Data-Labels**.

2. A submenu appears that offers labelling choices. Choose **A** to **F**, or **Group**, to assign labels to one of the six data ranges, or all ranges at once.

3. Answer the "Enter data-label range…" prompt by defining the range of cells that contain the labels to be used for identifying the points or bars on your graph.

4. Select **Center** to place the label directly on the data point. Select **Left**, **Right**, **Above**, or **Below** to place the label in the respective position to the left or right, or above or below, the data point itself.

5. Select **Quit** twice to return to the /Graph Main Menu.

See Also   /Graph X.

THE /GRAPH RESET COMMAND

● **PURPOSE**   To restore default values to some or all of the current graph's settings.

To Clear Data Ranges and Options Settings:

1.   Bring up the Main Menu and select **Graph**.

2.   Select **Reset** from the second-level menu.

3.   Select one choice from the third-level submenu that appears with settings that can be cleared or reset.

Graph—Clears all settings, restores all default values, saves all named graphs, and returns you to the /Graph menu.

X—Clears the X-range only.

A,B,C,D,E,F—Clears one data range and its associated labels.

Ranges—Clears all data ranges, X, and A–F, and any associated labels.

Options—Clears optional settings, such as legends.

Quit—Returns you to the /Graph menu.

See Also   /Graph Name

THE /GRAPH SAVE COMMAND

● **PURPOSE**   To save the current graph into a named disk file.

To Store a Graph as a .PIC File on Disk:

1. Bring up the Main Menu and select **Graph**.

2. Select **Save** from the second-level menu.

3. 1-2-3 switches to Files mode. Answer the "Enter graph file name" prompt by selecting one of the names from the list of files shown or by typing in a new name. 1-2-3 returns to the /Graph menu.

● **NOTES** When you save a graph with the /Graph Save command, a separate disk file with a .PIC extension is created to store the graph image. You can print the graph later with the PrintGraph program, or use it in another graphic processing program.

To save a graph within the current worksheet only, use the /Graph Name Create command. To store a .PIC version of more than one graph, change or restore the appropriate group of settings first. /Graph Save only stores the current settings as a .PIC file.

Examples

To store the current graph—obtainable by pressing F10—in a separately accessible .PIC file named CASHFLOW.PIC, select **/Graph Save**, type **CASHFLOW** in response to the prompt for a graph file name, and press ↵ to complete the operation and return to the /Graph menu.

See Also /Graph Name

THE /GRAPH TYPE COMMAND

● **PURPOSE** To select the kind of graph to create, or to add special features to the currently selected graph.

To Choose a Graph Type:

1. Bring up the Main Menu and select **Graph**.

2. Select **Type** from the second-level menu.

3. A third-level menu appears with eight choices:

Line—Specifies a line graph.

Bar—Specifies a bar graph.

XY—Specifies an XY plot.

Stack-Bar—Specifies a stacked bar graph.

Pie—Specifies a pie chart.

HLCO—Specifies a High-Low-Close-Open graph.

Mixed—Uses the A, B, C ranges for bars, and the D, E, F ranges for lines.

Features—Specifies one or more special graph characteristics.

To specify a particular graph type, select one of the first seven choices. 1-2-3 will return you to the /Graph menu.

To Create Special Graphical Effects:

1. Bring up the Main Menu and select **Graph**.

2. Select **Type** from the second-level menu.

3. A third-level menu appears. Select the eighth choice, **Features**.

4. 1-2-3 displays a submenu with five special graphing modifications:

Vertical—Draws an X-axis along the top of the graph.

Horizontal—Draws a Y-axis along the bottom of the graph.

Stacked—Draws all data ranges on top of one another.

Frame—Controls the appearance of graph frames, gutters, and zero lines.

3-D Effect—Creates a drop shadow behind your graph.

Select one of these options, or choose **Quit** to return to the /Graph menu.

THE /GRAPH VIEW COMMAND

● **PURPOSE**   To display an image of the currently defined graph.

To View the Current Graph:

1.   Bring up the Main Menu and select **Graph**.

2.   Select **View** from the second-level menu.

3.   1-2-3 draws the current graph, as specified in the Graph Settings box, on your screen. To remove this temporarily drawn graph, press any key to return to the /Graph menu.

● **NOTES**   As a shortcut for displaying the current graph, just press F10.

See Also   /Graph Name

THE /GRAPH X COMMAND

● **PURPOSE**   To define the range of cells to use for a graph's X-axis.

To Specify the X-axis Data Range:

1.   Bring up the Main Menu and select **Graph**.

2.   Select **X** from the second-level menu.

3.   Answer the "Enter X-axis range" prompt by using the arrow keys or mouse to identify the range of cells to use as the X-axis values.

4.   Press ↵ or click the mouse to complete the operation.

See Also   /Graph A (or B, C, D, E, or F).

THE ICONS ADD-IN (RELEASE 2.4)

● **PURPOSE**   To provide easy and colorful access to 1-2-3 and WYSIWYG commands and macros via a series of icons that represent predefined operations. The inside front and back covers of this book display and explain all available 1-2-3 *SmartIcons.*

To Use One of the Predefined SmartIcons:

With the Mouse:

1.   Move your mouse pointer to the desired SmartIcon from the current palette of icons seen on the right side of the screen.

2.   To display a different palette of icons, you can use your mouse to click on the right or left arrow at the bottom right of your screen. In between the two small arrows, 1-2-3 displays the current palette number.

3. Click once on the desired icon to run the macro or command represented by the icon.

With the keyboard:

1. First, invoke the ICONS add-in, then press the down arrow or up arrow to select a different icon on the currently displayed icon palette to the right of the worksheet. A blinking square moves to surround the currently selected icon.

2. Press the right or left arrow keys to display the next higher or next lower numbered palette. Then, move the blinking square to highlight an icon on that new palette.

3. Press ↵ to run the macro or command represented by the icon currently surrounded by a blinking square.

To Add an Icon to the Custom Palette (#1):

1. To add one of the existing icons to the custom palette, find the icon labelled "Add Icon" and select it.

2. Use the four arrow keys, as necessary, to highlight the icon that you would like copied to the bottom position in the custom palette. If you select an existing icon on palette #1, it will be moved to the bottom of the palette list.

3. Press ↵ to complete the copying (or moving) operation.

To Remove an Icon from the Custom Palette (#1):

1. To remove any single icon from the custom palette, find the icon labelled "Del Icon" and select it. The custom palette is then displayed.

2. Use the up and down arrow keys, as necessary, to highlight the icon that you would like to remove from the custom palette.

3. Press ↵ to complete the deletion operation.

To Assign a 1-2-3 or WYSIWYG
Command or Macro to a SmartIcon:

1. To assign any 1-2-3 or WYSIWYG command sequence, find the icon labelled "USER Icon" and select it. The User Icon Definitions window appears.

2. First, choose which of the twelve possible custom user icons you wish to define or redefine. To do this, click on U1 through U12; an asterisk appears beside the one you have chosen to work with. Keyboard users can select one of these by pressing Tab until the twelve choices in the Select Icon window are highlighted. Press the up or down arrow keys to move the asterisk to the User Defined Icon you wish to work with.

3. Next, press Tab to highlight the Define Icon pushbutton, and press ↵; or click on Define Icon with the mouse. The User-Defined Icon window appears.

4. Tab to the Icon Description field, or click on it with the mouse. Type in a description (up to 72 characters) of what your icon will do when later selected.

5. Move to the box labelled Get Macro Text From. To enter the desired commands or macro name from the keyboard, select Keyboard and press ↵. To use an existing group of macro instructions that can be found in the current worksheet, select Sheet and press ↵. Alternatively, you can click once on Keyboard or Sheet.

6. If you selected Keyboard in step 5, move to the Icon Macro Text field and type in a string (up to 240 characters) of macro commands. If you selected Sheet in step 5, move to the Range field and type in a cell range, a valid range name, or an existing macro name.

7. Choose OK to return to the User Icon Definitions window.

8. Choose OK again to restore your worksheet and complete the icon (re)definition procedure.

• **NOTES**   You must first use the /Add-In Attach menu choice
to load ICONS into memory. By default, 1-2-3 Release 2.4 automatically attaches the ICONS add-in, using Alt-F7 as the shortcut key.
You can run the program with the /Add-In Invoke command, or by
pressing Alt-F7. ICONS is only available in 1-2-3 Release 2.4.

When a new icon is added to the custom palette, it is always added
at the bottom of the existing list. If the custom palette is completely
full, the bottom icon is replaced by your latest addition. If you wish
to move any icon on the custom palette down to the bottom position, simply use the "Add Icon" mechanism, and select that icon
from the custom palette itself. The selected icon moves to the bottom of the custom palette when you press ↵.

To clear all macro and user icon definitions, choose the Clear All
Icons pushbutton on the User Icon Definitions window; then press
OK. You can still cancel this clearing effect by choosing Cancel on
this window prior to pressing OK.

Examples

To define User Icon #1 as the equivalent of a /Range Format Currency, with no decimal places, first select the "USER Icon" icon. In
the User Icon Definitions window that appears, choose U1 so
that the asterisk appears beside it. Then press the Define Icon
pushbutton.

In the User-Defined Icon window that next appears, type the following description into the Icon Description field:

Format as currency with no decimal places

Select Keyboard in the Get Macro Text From field. Then, type the
following macro instructions into the Icon Macro Text field:

/RFC0~~

Choose OK twice to return to your worksheet. Find and select the icon labelled "Add Icon". Move the highlight to the U1 icon and press ↵. Your currency formatting icon is now available on your custom palette.

See Also   / Add-In Attach, / Add-In Invoke, BSOLVER, MAC-ROMGR, TUTOR, VIEWER, WYSIWYG

THE MACROMGR ADD-IN

● **PURPOSE**   To extend the power of 1-2-3 by managing libraries of frequently used data and programmed instruction sequences, or macros.

To Load a Specific Macro Library:

1.   Bring up the MACROMGR Main Menu and select **Load**.

2.   1-2-3 switches to Files mode. Answer the "Enter name of macro library to load" prompt by selecting one of the names from the list of .MLB files shown or by typing a different pathname.

3.   If the library name already exists in memory, you will be asked if you want to overwrite it with the named .MLB disk file. Select **No** to cancel the request and return to Ready mode; or select **Yes** to read the specified file into memory.

Macro libraries are stored in .MLB files and can contain macros or any other worksheet data. Once you load it, a library is stored in a memory area separate from your worksheet. You can load up to ten libraries into memory at the same time.

To Store a Cell Range in a Macro Library:

1. Bring up the MACROMGR Main Menu and select **Save**.

2. 1-2-3 switches to Files mode. Answer the "Enter name of macro library to save" prompt by selecting one of the names from the list of .MLB files shown or by typing a different file name.

    a. If you selected a file name that already exists on disk (and possibly in memory as well), you will be asked if you want to overwrite the file's contents with a new range of cells. Select **No** to cancel the request and return to Ready mode; or **Yes** to continue with the Save process.

3. Answer the "Enter macro library range" prompt by identifying the range of cells that is to constitute the contents of the macro library named in step 2.

4. Select **No** if you wish to allow others to be able to edit your macro library. 1-2-3 returns you immediately to Ready mode.

5. Select **Yes** to password-protect the library and allow only those who know the password to edit its contents.

6. You are asked to enter a password. Type in any combination of 80 or fewer characters and press ⏎ or click the mouse to complete the operation and return to Ready mode.

You can assign a library the name AUTOLOAD.MLB and have 1-2-3 automatically read it into memory whenever you attach the MACROMGR. Remember to define the range to include all cells referred to in any formulas within the range.

To keep your system's memory consumption to a minimum, define as few empty cells as possible within the range. Do this because 1-2-3 reserves as many cells in conventional memory as there are cells in the library range.

To Read and Edit
the Contents of a Macro Library:

1. Bring up the MACROMGR Main Menu and select **Edit**.

2. 1-2-3 switches to Names mode and displays the names of any libraries currently in memory. Answer the "Enter name of macro library to edit" prompt by selecting a library name.

3. Tell 1-2-3 how to resolve named range conflicts by selecting

   • **Ignore** to use range names from the worksheet; or

   • **Overwrite** to use range names from the macro library.

4. Answer the "Enter range for macro library" prompt by identifying the top-left corner cell of the worksheet where you want MACROMGR to begin writing the library contents.

5. Press ↵ or click the mouse to copy the contents of the library into your worksheet and return to Ready mode.

As you edit a macro library, remember that the original version remains unchanged both on disk and in memory. You are only adjusting a worksheet copy of the macro library. After you've modified it, select the Save choice to store the corrected copy.

Use the Save and Edit choices to create a cut-and-paste facility for worksheet data. For example, you could store a useful table of data or formulas in a macro library and use the Edit command later on to paste it into other worksheets you've retrieved into memory.

To Free the Memory Used by a Macro Library:

1. Bring up the MACROMGR Main Menu and select **Remove**.

2. 1-2-3 switches to Names mode and displays the names of any libraries currently in memory. Answer the "Enter name of macro library to remove" prompt by selecting a name.

3. Press ⏎ or click the mouse to complete the operation and return to Ready mode.

To Obtain a List of Range Names in a Macro Library:

1. Bring up the MACROMGR Main Menu and select **Name-List**.

2. 1-2-3 switches to Names mode and displays the names of any libraries currently in memory. Answer the "Enter macro library name" prompt by selecting a name.

3. Answer the "Enter range for list" prompt by specifying the top cell of a blank column. MACROMGR will write a single-column table of range names used in the library.

4. Press ⏎ or click the mouse to complete the operation and return to READY mode.

● **NOTES**   You must first use the /Add-In Attach menu choice to load MACROMGR into memory and run the program with the /Add-In Invoke command. Alternatively, you can press one of four possible Alt-function key combinations if you made Alt-function key assignments during the /Add-In Attach process. Select Quit to return to READY mode.

Examples

Suppose you've written a number of worksheets and have just learned how to control the date and time indicator on the bottom line of your screen. Now that you understand how to switch the display from Date/Time to Filename and back, you want to have this ability each time you work with a worksheet. The command to switch to Filename display is /Worksheet Global Default Other Clock Filename Quit. The command to switch back to Date/Time display is /Worksheet Global Default Other Clock Clock Quit. Rather than selecting the long menu choice each time, you write two simple macros on a blank worksheet: Alt-F to switch to Filename indication, and Alt-D to switch back to Date/Time indication.

With your two macros located in cells C3..E10, bring up the MAC-ROMGR and select **Save**; specify STATLINE as the library name; indicate C3..E10 as the range to write into the library, and respond **No** to the password query. Now, the macros are erased from the original worksheet and stored in the STATLINE.MLB file.

To test new macros, you use **/File Retrieve** to bring each of your existing worksheets into memory; bring up the MACROMGR and select **Edit**; select STATLINE.MLB as the library to use; choose **Ignore** as the range name resolution method; and choose a blank area of each worksheet into which to read the macros. If, after you've copied the library into your worksheet, you discover that \F or \D do not switch to Filename or Date/Time display mode, you must have a pre-existing macro in the worksheet with the same name.

See Also   /Add-In Attach, /Add-In Invoke, AUDITOR, BSOLVER, ICONS, TUTOR, VIEWER, and WYSIWYG.

THE /MOVE COMMAND

● **PURPOSE**   To transfer both cell formats and cell contents from one worksheet location to another.

To Move One or More Cells to Another Worksheet Location:

1.   Bring up the Main Menu and select **Move**.

2.   Answer the "Move what?" prompt by using the arrow keys or mouse to identify the range of cells to be relocated.

3.   Answer the "To where?" prompt by positioning the cell pointer where you want the original cells to go.

4.   Press ↵ or click the mouse to complete the operation.

• NOTES   When you move data, all formulas that reference the data are automatically adjusted. When you move formulas, all cell references are rewritten to refer to the same data. Both cell contents and formatting are moved during the operation. To replicate a cell and its formatting without erasing the original data, use the /Copy command.

A range of cells being moved is placed in its new location beginning at the top-left corner of the range, regardless of how you defined the range being moved.

Examples

Suppose that you've been keeping track of invoices received in chronological order. However, you suddenly receive an invoice dated two months ago. You could enter it and resort all your worksheet rows, or you could move a range of cells downward and free the space to type in the new invoice's information.

Let's say that your invoice data occupies columns A to F and you have 60 invoices stored in a worksheet. If your worksheet has several macros defined just to the right in columns I to K, you may not want to use the /Worksheet Insert command because it would destroy the integrity of one of the macros. To insert the new invoice information just after row seven, move the cell pointer to cell A8 and select **/Move**. In response to the "Move What?" prompt, extend the cell highlight to include A8..F60 and press ⏎. Next, to answer the "To Where?" prompt, move the cell pointer to cell A9 and press ⏎. The entire block of invoice data is moved down by one cell, opening up a line of empty cells for the invoice data.

See Also   /Copy

THE /PRINT BACKGROUND COMMAND

• **PURPOSE**   To make a copy of the printout in an encoded file, and to print that file while other 1-2-3 operations continue.

To Print Part or All of a Worksheet in the Background:

1.   Bring up the Main Menu and select **Print**.

2.   Select **Background** from the second-level menu.

3.   1-2-3 switches to Files mode. Answer the "Enter name of background print file" prompt by selecting a name from the list of .ENC files shown or by typing a new file name to receive the encoded print output.

   a.   If you selected a name that already exists on disk, you will be asked if you want to overwrite the file's contents with the new encoded output that will be sent to the disk file. Select **Cancel** to withdraw the printing request and return to Ready mode; or select **Replace** to continue with the printing request and display the Print Settings Main Menu.

4.   To tell 1-2-3 the nature of your worksheet data and how you want it to appear when printed, follow the instructions beginning at step 3 of the /Print Printer command below.

• **NOTES**   /Print Background enables 1-2-3 to print a file while you continue doing other operations. The file is said to be printed "in the background" and your other tasks are said to be performed "in the foreground."   1-2-3 asks you to specify all the same printing parameters you specify for other printing operations. The output data is merged into a named file along with the printer control codes, which is why the file is called "encoded." The Background Print (BPRINT) program manages the print process while 1-2-3 continues to manage your other requests.

Prior to using the /Print Background command, you must have initiated the BPRINT program from the original operating system prompt. Do not use the /System command to run the BPRINT program.

Examples

To create an encoded file named CASHFLOW.ENC and print it in the background so you don't have to wait to do other work, select **/Print Background** and type CASHFLOW.ENC. When the Print Settings menu appears, specify all relevant factors and then **Go** to create the file and **Quit** to print it.

See Also   /Print File and /Print Printer.

THE /PRINT ENCODED COMMAND

● **PURPOSE**   To create a file with data and codes for printing on a different printer later on.

To Encode Print Information for a Different System Printer:

1.   Bring up the Main Menu and select **Print**.

2.   Select **Encoded** from the second-level menu.

3.   1-2-3 switches to Files mode. Answer the "Enter name of encoded file" prompt by selecting a name from the list of

.ENC files shown or by typing a new file name to receive the encoded print output.

a. If you selected a file that already exists on disk, you will be asked if you want to overwrite the file's contents with the new encoded output that will be sent to the disk file. Select **Cancel** to withdraw the printing request and return to Ready mode; or select **Replace** to continue with the printing request and display the Print Settings Main Menu.

4. To tell 1-2-3 the nature of your worksheet data and how you want it to appear when printed, continue with the instructions in step 3 of the /Print Printer command below.

● **NOTES** Use /Print Encoded to prepare a file for printing on a different system's printer. Be sure to issue the /Worksheet Global Default Printer Name command to make the anticipated printer into the current one on your system. This way, 1-2-3 can embed the correct printer codes into the encoded file that will be created.

Later, use your operating system's Copy command to print the encoded file on another computer system. In fact, as long as the correct printer is connected, you can even print the encoded file on your own system. If you use Copy, be sure to include the /B switch. For example, to print an encoded file named CASHFLOW.ENC later on to the LPT1 port, you could simply enter

COPY CASHFLOW.ENC/B LPT1:

If you are no longer using 1-2-3, you can continue doing other work on your system and use 1-2-3's background printing program, BPRINT, to print the same file by entering this command:

BPRINT CASHFLOW.ENC

Examples

To create an encoded file named CASHFLOW.ENC and be able to print it later with your own system printer, select **/Print Encoded** and type CASHFLOW.ENC. When the Print Settings menu appears, specify all relevant factors and then choose **Go** to begin creating the file and **Quit** to return to Ready mode. After you exit 1-2-3, and before you initiate another major program on your system, you can start the background printing of the file by typing BPRINT CASHFLOW.ENC at the operating system prompt.

See Also   /Worksheet Global

THE /PRINT
FILE COMMAND

● **PURPOSE**   To create a formatted ASCII text file containing selected 1-2-3 data.

To Send ASCII Print
Information to a Text File on Disk:

1.   Bring up the Main Menu and select **Print**.

2.   Select **File** from the second-level menu.

3.   1-2-3 switches to Files mode. Answer the "Enter name of text file" prompt by selecting a name from the list of .PRN files shown or by typing a new file name to receive the text characters output by 1-2-3.

    a. If you select a name that already exists on disk, you will be asked if you want to overwrite its file contents with the new encoded output that 1-2-3 will send to the disk file. Select **Cancel** to withdraw the printing request and return to Ready mode; or select **Replace** to continue with the printing request and display the Print Settings Main Menu.

4.   To tell 1-2-3 the nature of your worksheet data and how you want it to appear when printed, follow the instructions beginning at step 3 of the /Print Printer command below.

• **NOTES**   Use /Print File when you want to remove control characters from data and export it in its most easily manipulated form. The data is not printed, but it is available for access by other programs or can be printed at another time. To strip off page breaks, headers, and footers from the output, use the /Print File Options Other Unformatted command. To keep blank lines and truncated long lines to a minimum, use the /Print File Options Margins None command.

Examples

Suppose you want to export an inventory database of 2500 rows and include it in a specially formatted printout that will be combined with some word-processed company information. First, you would issue the **/Print File Options Margins None** command to eliminate blank margin lines at the top and bottom of pages. Then you would remove form feed codes and extra header and footer lines with the **/Print File Options Other Unformatted** command. You would select **/Print File** to specify a file name such as INVENT and define all the necessary Print Settings. Finally, you would choose **Go** to direct the text output to the INVENT.PRN file.

See Also   /File Import

THE /PRINT PRINTER COMMAND

• **PURPOSE**   To print a range of data on your system's printer.

To Initiate the /Print Printer Command:

1.   Bring up the Main Menu and select **Print**.

2. Select **Printer** from the second-level menu.

3. A third-level menu appears with the following choices:

Range Line Page Options Clear Align Go Quit

Select one choice according to the action you wish to perform.

The principal choices—**Range**, **Options**, and **Clear**—are explained in the subsequent sections. Simple preparatory steps also include:

- **Line**, which advances the paper by one line;

- **Page**, which advances the paper to the top of the next page; and

- **Align**, which tells 1-2-3 that you've adjusted the paper to the top of a page.

After selecting appropriate preparatory choices, you may choose **Go** to initiate the actual printout on your system printer. Finally, choose **Quit** on this menu to return to the preceding /Print menu.

To Specify a Range of Cells to Print:

1. From the Print Settings Menu, choose **Range**.

2. Answer the "Enter print range" prompt by using your keyboard or mouse to define the range of cells you want 1-2-3 to include in the type of output you've requested.

3. Press ↵ or click the mouse to return to the Print Settings Menu.

To Define Headers and Footers:

1. From the Print Settings menu, choose **Options**.

2. From the Options menu, select

    a. **Header** to specify a line of text to appear just below the top margin on each page. Next, type in a line of text. It can be up to 240 characters long.

    b. **Footer** to specify a line of text to appear just above the bottom margin on each page. Next, type in a line of text. It can be up to 240 characters long.

3. Press ↵ or click the mouse to return to the Options menu.

You can include special characters inside headers or footers. Furthermore, by entering an AT (@) sign, you can have 1-2-3 enter the current date from the system clock; a number (#) sign enters the current page number; and broken verticals (¦) separate text into left-, center-, and right-aligned portions of the line. Also, by entering a backslash followed by a cell identifier, you can have 1-2-3 enter a cell's contents in a header or footer line.

To Define Page Margins:

1. From the Print Settings menu, choose **Options**.

2. From the Options menu, select **Margins**.

3. From the Margins menu, select

    a. **Left** or **Right** to set the side margins. Enter a value between 0 and 240.

    b. **Top** or **Bottom** to set the upper and lower margins of the printed page. Enter a value between 0 and 32.

    c. **None** to set the top, bottom, and left margins to zero, and the right margin to 240.

4. Press ↵ or click the mouse to return to the Options menu.

Top and bottom margin numbers are counted in lines, and the default for both values is 2. Left and right margin settings are both counted in characters from the left margin, and the default values are 4 and 76. Remember to change the left and right margins whenever you change the pitch, or font, for your printer. You may have to do this after a special setup string is sent from 1-2-3, or after a front panel request on your printer.

To Specify Column or Row Borders:

1. From the Print Settings menu, choose **Options**.

2. Select **Borders** from the second-level menu.

3. From the Borders menu, select

    a. **Columns** to print one or more worksheet columns on each page to the left of the selected print range.

    b. **Rows** to print one or more worksheet rows on each page just above the selected print range.

4. Answer the "Enter range for border columns (or rows)" prompt by using the keyboard or mouse to define the vertical (or horizontal) range of cells to use.

5. Press ⏎ or click the mouse to return to the Options menu.

Do not include the border cells as part of the range you indicate in the Print Settings choices. If you do, those cells will print twice.

To Define a Printer Setup String:

1. From the Print Settings menu, choose **Options**.

2. Select **Setup** from the second-level menu.

3. Answer the "Enter setup string" prompt by typing a string up to 39 control characters long that begins with a backslash.

4. Press ⏎ or click the mouse to return to the Options menu.

To include an unprintable code, use the three-digit ASCII decimal equivalent.

To Define the Number
of Lines Per Printed Page:

1. From the Print Settings menu, choose **Options**.

2. Select **Pg-Length** from the second-level menu.

3. Answer the "Enter lines per page (1..100)" prompt by typing a value between one and a hundred.

4. Press ⏎ or click the mouse to return to the Options menu.

From the number you enter in step 3, 1-2-3 subtracts three lines for a reserved header area, three lines for a reserved footer area, and the values set for the top and bottom margins. The number of lines that remains represents data lines to be printed on each output page.

If you change lines-per-inch setting in your printer (either with a setup string or other hardware mechanism), be sure to change the Pg-Length option appropriately. Larger or smaller fonts will, respectively, reduce or expand the number of lines that can fit on a piece of paper. Also, smaller or larger forms than the standard 8.5"× 11" paper require changes to the Pg-Length setting.

To List Cell Formulas Rather than Cell Values:

1. From the Print Settings menu, choose **Options**.

2. Select **Other** from the second-level menu.

3. From the menu of Other options, choose **Cell-Formulas**.

4. Press ⏎ or click the mouse to return to the Options menu.

When you print with this option selected, 1-2-3 prints one line of output for each line in your worksheet. Each line contains the standard control panel data for each cell: its address, format, protection status, and contents.

To Remove Headers, Footers, Top and Bottom Margins, and Page Breaks from a Printout:

1. From the Print Settings menu, choose **Options**.

2. Select **Other** from the second-level menu.

3. From the menu of Other options, choose **Unformatted**.

4. Press ↵ or click the mouse to return to the Options menu.

Select this option when you want to export data to other programs and eliminate the extraneous blank lines that separate portions of your actual worksheet data.

Examples

Suppose your worksheet contains ID, NAME, PAYRATE, and STATUS information for all employees, and these four capitalized labels head columns A to D. You could print a list of all employees by selecting **/Print Printer**. To ensure that the four labels in cells A3..D3 appear at the top of each page's output, select **Options Borders Rows** and specify A3..D3 as the borders row range to repeat at the top of each page. Next, select **Quit** on the Options menu and select **Align Go** to print the employee information. The column labels will repeat on each page.

See Also   /Print Background

THE /QUIT COMMAND

● **PURPOSE**   To end a 1-2-3 work session.

To Return to DOS,
or to the Lotus Access System Menu:

1.   Bring up the Main Menu and select **Quit**.

2.   A confirmation menu appears. Choose either

    a. **No** to withdraw the request and return to READY mode; or

    b. **Yes** to exit 1-2-3.

3.   If you made changes to the current worksheet and have not yet saved them, 1-2-3 will alert you to this fact with a final confirmation request.

    a. Choose **No** to withdraw your exit request and return to Ready mode, or

    b. Choose **Yes** to exit 1-2-3 and discard the most recent changes t your worksheet.

● **NOTES**   Use the /File Save command to save your work before you exit 1-2-3 and return to the operating system prompt to do other work.

See Also   /File Save and /System.

THE /RANGE
ERASE COMMAND

● **PURPOSE**   To clear a cell or an entire range of cells.

To Erase the Contents of One or More Cells:

1.   Bring up the Main Menu and select **Range**.

2.   Select **Erase** from the second-level menu.

3. Answer the "Enter range to erase" prompt by using the keyboard or mouse to define the block of cells to erase.

4. Press ↵ or click the mouse to complete the operation.

● **NOTES**   This command removes data only from unprotected cells. Protect your worksheet to prevent accidental data erasure. Range names are not affected by this command, and neither is the formatting and protection status of the cells. To erase a single cell, simply press the Del key. To erase one or more entire columns or rows of cells, use /Worksheet Delete. To erase an entire worksheet, use /Worksheet Erase.

Examples

Suppose you used a small block of cells (C3..D6) as a scratch pad while talking with a client. After the discussions were completed, you could erase the data still in those cells by selecting **/Range Erase** and specifying C3..D6 as the range to erase.

See Also   /File Erase, /Worksheet Erase, and /Worksheet Delete.

THE /RANGE FORMAT COMMAND

● **PURPOSE**   To define the appearance of the data in one or more cells.

To Initiate the /Range Format Command:

1. Bring up the Main Menu and select **Range**.

2. Select **Format** from the second-level menu.

3.   A third-level menu appears with the following choices:

Fixed Sci Currency , General +/– Percent Date
Text Hidden Reset

Select one choice according to the action you wish to
perform.

The principal choices are explained in the subsequent sections.
Choose Reset on this menu to restore specified cells to their original
global formats.

To Choose a Numeric
Format for a Range of Cells:

1.   After you've selected the /**Range Format** command,
choose one of the following options:

Fixed—Displays zero to fifteen decimal places, leading
zeros, and a minus sign for negative numbers.
Example: 34.756

Sci—Displays numbers in exponential format, allowing a
mantissa of zero to fifteen decimal places, and an ex-
ponent that ranges from –99 to +99.
Example: 23.3456E–45

Currency—Displays trailing zeros, a leading currency symbol, commas to separate thousands, and zero to fifteen decimal places. Also encloses negative numbers in parentheses.
Example: 3956.50

General—Displays a minus sign for negative values, but
no commas or trailing zeros (this is the default notation).
Example: 3956.5

2.   Answer the "Enter range to format" prompt by using
the keyboard or mouse to define a range of cells that will
be assigned the numeric format specified in step 1.

3.   Press ↵ or click the mouse to complete the operation.

1-2-3 automatically switches from General format to Sci format
when the integer portion of the number exceeds the current

column's width. If the decimal portion of a number exceeds the current column's width, the value will appear truncated. 1-2-3 will maintain the precise value for subsequent calculations, however.

To Choose Date and Time Formats for a Range of Cells:

1. Select the **/Range Format** command and choose **Date**.

2. Select one of the following formats, according to how you want the date values to appear:

1	The dd-mmm-yy standard long date format.
2	The dd-mmm standard short date format.
3	The mmm-yy standard short date format.
4	The long international system date format, the appearance of which depends on how your system is configured. The default is mm/dd/yy.
5	The short international system date format. The default is mm/dd.
Time	One of four time formats.

Choose the time format from the following submenu:

- **1** is the standard hh:mm:ss AM/PM format.
- **2** is the standard hh:mm AM/PM format.
- **3** is the currently configured long international format.
- **4** is the currently configured short international format.

3. Answer the "Enter range to format" prompt by using the keyboard or mouse to define a range of cells whose date values will be displayed in the specified date or time format.

4. Press ↵ or click the mouse to complete the operation.

To set the default long or short international format for date/time, use the /Worksheet Global Default Other International Date/Time command. The integer portion of date values ranges from 1 (representing January 1, 1900) to 73050 (representing December 31, 2099). The decimal portion of the same date values ranges from .000000 (representing 12:00:00 AM) to .999999 (representing 12:00:00 PM).

To Display Text Formulas Instead of Resulting Values:

1. Select the **/Range Format** command and choose **Text**.

2. Answer the "Enter range to format" prompt by using the keyboard or mouse to define a range of cells whose formula contents will be displayed as text in those cells.

3. Press ↵ or click the mouse to complete the operation.

When cells are formatted as Text, their values are displayed in General format and their formulas are displayed as themselves, not as computed results.

To Hide the Contents of a Cell:

1. Select the **/Range Format** command and choose **Hidden**.

2. Answer the "Enter range to format" prompt by using the keyboard or mouse to define a range of cells whose contents can't be viewed or printed.

3. Press ↵ or click the mouse to complete the operation.

To guarantee that hidden cells are not accidentally overwritten or erased, protect the worksheet with the /Worksheet Global Protection command. To redisplay hidden cells, use /Range Format Reset or simply change formats to something other than Hidden. To check the contents of a hidden cell, move the cell pointer to it and observe the contents in the control panel. To hide an entire column, use the /Worksheet Column Hide command.

Examples

Suppose that column C (from C4..C250) contains salary figures for all your employees. To format this column as Currency with two decimal places, select **/Range Format Currency 2** and specify C4..C250. If asterisks appear, widen the column with the /Worksheet Column Set-Width command.

See Also   /Range Search, /Worksheet Global, and @INT.

THE /RANGE INPUT COMMAND

● **PURPOSE**   To restrict data entry only to cells in a range that is unprotected.

To Limit Data Entry to Specific Cells in a Range:

1. Bring up the Main Menu and select **Range**.

2. Select **Input** from the second-level menu.

3. Answer the "Enter data input range" prompt by using the keyboard or mouse to specify the block of cells to be considered during input operations.

4. If there are unprotected cells in the protected range, the cell pointer moves to the first one. Enter or edit data in that cell, and the cell pointer moves to the next unprotected cell. Press the arrow keys to continue entering or editing data or formulas in the unprotected cells. 1-2-3 does not move the cell pointer to any cell which has not been unprotected.

5. Press **Esc** to exit from Restricted Input Processing mode and return to Ready mode.

● **NOTES**   Use this command for convenience when you enter or edit data on fill-in-the-blanks forms. It can be especially helpful during interactive macros. First protect the overall worksheet, and then unprotect only the cells to be used for data entry. The protected cells contain labels and data to remain visible but unchanged; the unprotected cells afford users an opportunity to enter or edit only what is required.

Use the /Worksheet Global Protection command to protect the entire worksheet. Use the /Range Unprot command to unprotect certain cells for data entry.

Examples

Suppose you are using your own worksheet to prepare a 1040 income tax form. In order to understand which lines you are completing, you copy all the labels from the IRS form(s). Next you protect the entire worksheet and unprotect the cells into which you must enter numbers, such as wages earned and taxes withheld. You select **/Range Input** and specify the entire range of labels, formulas, and data entry cells. Each time you press the ↓ key, 1-2-3 moves the cell pointer past all the label and formula cells. You can quickly enter numbers into only those few cells that are necessary to income tax preparation. Press **Esc** when you're done. Print your results, mail the information, and wait for your refund.

See Also   /Range Unprot and /Worksheet Global.

THE /RANGE JUSTIFY COMMAND

● **PURPOSE**   To specify a column width for a vertical range of long labels.

To Condense the On-Screen Appearance of a Column of Long Labels:

1. Move the cell pointer to the top cell in a column of long labels to be justified.

2. Bring up the Main Menu and select **Range**.

3. Select **Justify** from the second-level menu.

4. Answer the "Enter justify range" prompt by using the keyboard or mouse to specify a range whose width will dictate the left- and right-justification boundaries.

5. Press ↵ or click the mouse to complete the operation.

● **NOTES**   All labels, beginning at the specified cell and continuing down the column up to the first blank or numeric cell, are rewritten into the same column. However, the rewritten labels use a width that equals the sum of the column widths in the specified justify range.

Examples

Suppose that you have a single long label in cell A1:

**Now is the time for all good men to come to the aid of
their country.**

and that column A has a width of 32 characters. Move the cell pointer to A1 and select **/Range Justify**. 1-2-3 rewrites this label into cells A1..A3 as

**Now is the time for all good
men to come to the aid of their
country.**

See Also   /Worksheet Global

THE /RANGE
LABEL COMMAND

● **PURPOSE**   To control the positioning of labels in a cell range.

To Specify Label Alignment in Cells:

1.   Bring up the Main Menu and select **Range**.

2.   Select **Label** from the second-level menu.

3.   Select one of three label alignments:

Left—Places the label beginning at the leftmost character position in the cell.

Right—Places the label ending at the rightmost character position in the cell.

Center—Positions the label in the center of the cell.

4. Answer the "Enter range of labels" prompt by using the keyboard or mouse to specify a range of cells to be affected.

5. Press ↵ or click the mouse to complete the operation.

● **NOTES** This command only affects existing labels; it changes the alignment prefix of all labels within the range you specify. However, the command cannot preset an alignment in a cell.

Examples

Suppose row F7..F20 contained the headings of data categories in your worksheet. As you were building your worksheet, you typed the titles into their cells, so they are left-justified by default. However, when you entered the numeric data, which is automatically right-justified, into the columns, you realized that right-aligned labels would look better.

You could select **/Range Label Right** and specify F7..F20 as the range to adjust. Now all of the apostrophe (') prefixes would be replaced immediately with quotes (") and the labels aligned to the right of each row F cell.

See Also /Worksheet Global

THE /RANGE NAME COMMAND

● **PURPOSE** To assign a name to a cell range.

To Initiate the /Range Name Command:

1. Bring up the Main Menu and select **Range**.

2. Select **Name** from the second-level menu that appears.

3. Make one choice from the third-level menu:

Create   Delete   Labels   Reset   Table

The principal choices are explained in the subsequent sections. To use an existing range of labels to automatically create a set of range names, select **Labels**. Choose **Reset** to delete all existing range names.

To Create or Modify a Range Name:

1. From the /Range Name submenu, choose **Create**.

2. 1-2-3 switches to Edit mode if no named ranges exist yet: otherwise it switches to Names mode and displays existing range names on line three. Answer the "Enter name" prompt by selecting an existing name to modify or by typing in a new name in order to create a new named range.

3. Answer the "Enter range" prompt by using the keyboard or mouse to define the cell range being named.

4. Press ↵ or click the mouse to complete the operation.

Range names can be as many as fifteen characters long, but may not include any spaces or any of these characters:

+   *   –   /   &   >   <   @   #   {   ,   ;

1-2-3 does not differentiate between upper- and lowercase characters in a range name, but it can become confused in formulas with range names that begin with digits. Use characters in range names that are easy to read and work with. In addition, do not select range names that can be confused with cell addresses (such as D7), macro names, function names, or 1-2-3 reserved names.

To Delete a Range Name:

1. From the /Range Name submenu, choose **Delete**.

2. 1-2-3 switches to Names mode—if named ranges exist—
and displays range names on line three. Answer the
"Enter name to delete" prompt by selecting a name to
remove.

3. Press ↵ or click the mouse to complete the operation.

When you delete a range name, only the name is removed from
your worksheet. The data in the named range is not affected at all.
Formulas that used the range name are rewritten automatically to
refer to the actual cell addresses.

To Generate a Table
of Existing Range Names:

1. From the /Range Name submenu, select **Table**.

2. Answer the "Enter range for table" prompt by moving the
cell pointer to a blank portion of your worksheet.

3. Press ↵ or click the mouse. 1-2-3 writes the table in
two columns, using the top-left corner of the range
you specified as the top-left corner of the table.

Use this command to both document and possibly debug your
worksheet. The resulting table contains two columns; one for the
range name itself and the other for the range that is named.

Examples

Suppose that your worksheet summarizes income projections for
four fiscal quarters and stores the totals in cells F13..F16. Just to the
left of these values, you have entered four labels ("Q1", "Q2", "Q3",
"Q4") as documentation. In subsequent formulas for analysis, you
would like to refer to each referenced quarter by name.

Select **/Range Name Labels Right**. Specify E13..E16 as the location
of the labels to use. 1-2-3 quickly creates all four named ranges,

using each label in column E as the name of the adjacent cell in column F.

THE /RANGE PROT COMMAND

● **PURPOSE**   To protect cells in a protected worksheet that were previously unprotected.

To Turn Protection On for One or More Cells:

1.   Bring up the Main Menu and select **Range**.

2.   Select **Prot** from the second-level menu.

3.   Answer the "Enter range to protect" prompt by using the keyboard or mouse to specify a range of cells to be protected.

4.   Press ⏎ or click the mouse to complete the operation.

● **NOTES**   Use the /Range Prot command to turn cell protection back on for the specified cells. This command is only meaningful if the /Worksheet Global Protection command is enabled; only cells that have been subsequently unprotected with /Range Unprot are affected. 1-2-3 does not allow you to edit, erase, copy, move, insert, or delete rows or columns in a protected worksheet.

Examples

Suppose that your worksheet is globally protected, and while you have been waiting for new government regulations to be printed you have left cell G7 unprotected to allow others to enter a discounting factor there. Now that you have the information you've been waiting for, you have replaced G7 with a formula that does a table lookup to obtain the correct discount factor. Select **/Range Prot** and specify cell G7 as the cell to once again protect. Now your formula is protected from accidental modification, and any /Range Input macros will no longer move the cell pointer to the G7 address.

See Also /Range Unprot and /Worksheet Global.

THE /RANGE SEARCH COMMAND

● **PURPOSE** To discover which cell labels or formulas contain a specified string.

To Search through Formulas/Labels in a Range for a Specified String:

1. Bring up the Main Menu and select **Range**.

2. Select **Search** from the second-level menu.

3. Answer the "Enter range to search" prompt by using the keyboard or mouse to specify a range of cells to be considered.

4. Answer the "Enter string to search for" prompt by typing a combination of characters to find.

5. From the submenu that appears, select an option to tell 1-2-3 where to look for the specified string:

Formulas—Looks for the string within formulas only.

Labels—Looks for the string within labels only.

Both—Looks for the string within both labels and formulas.

6. From the submenu that appears, choose either **Find** to highlight each occurrence of the search string in succession; or **Replace** to change each occurrence of the search string to another character string.

a. If you select **Find**, choose **Next** to highlight each succeeding occurrence of the specified search string, and, when you're done, **Quit** to return to Ready mode.

b. If you select **Replace**, you next type the replacement string and press ↵. From the submenu that appears, you must tell 1-2-3 which occurrences of the search string are to be replaced:

- **Replace** changes the occurrence and moves to the next one.

- **All** changes all occurrences from the location of the cell pointer to the end of the search range.

- **Next** does not change this highlighted occurrence, but skips to the next one.

- **Quit** returns to Ready mode.

7. When 1-2-3 can find no more occurrences, it displays an error window on screen. Press **Esc** to return to Ready mode.

● **NOTES**   1-2-3 treats numbers in search strings as characters only. You can find character occurrences within labels or formulas, but not within numeric value cells.

Examples

Suppose column G in your customer contacts database table contains phone numbers and the phone company announces a new Boston area code. You can select **/Range Search** to change the affected 617 area codes to 508. If the area codes are enclosed in parentheses, specify all of column G as the range to search, (617) as the string to search for, **Labels** as the type of data to search, and **Replace** as the mode to use. When 1-2-3 asks you for a replacement string, type (**508**). As 1-2-3 finds each occurrence, choose **Replace** to change the area code, **Next** to skip the individual occurrence, or **All** to replace all matching strings with the replacement string.

See Also   /Range Format and /Worksheet Column.

THE /RANGE TRANS COMMAND

● **PURPOSE**   To reverse rows with columns in a specified range, and to replace formulas with current values.

To Transpose the Columns and Rows of a Specified Range:

1. Bring up the Main Menu and select **Range**.

2. Select **Trans** from the second-level menu.

3. Answer the "Transpose what?" prompt by using the keyboard or mouse to specify a range of cells.

4. Answer the "To where?" prompt by moving the cell pointer to the upper-left corner cell in the destination range.

5. Press ↵ or click the mouse to complete the operation.

● **NOTES**   Column and row entries in the transpose range are reversed in the destination range. In the process, formulas are not copied; instead, current values are written into the destination cells.

Examples

Let's say cell range E13..F16 contains four fiscal quarter results, column E contains labels, and column F contains summation formulas. Your boss complains because she likes to see quarterly figures in their own columns. While she watches, you select **/Range Trans**, you specify E13..F16 as the transpose range, move the cell pointer to G13, and press ↵. The result in cells G13..J14 is

Q1	Q2	Q3	Q4
$2,345	$4,557	$5,343	$3,566

Note that the dollar values in cells G14..J14 are actual numbers; these cells do not contain formulas that would be updated by changes to the original cells on which the formulas in column F depend.

See Also   /Copy, /File Admin, and /Range Value.

THE /RANGE UNPROT COMMAND

● **PURPOSE**   To unprotect individual cells in a protected worksheet.

To Remove Protection Selectively from Cells in a Protected Worksheet:

1. Bring up the Main Menu and select **Range**.

2. Select **Unprot** from the second-level menu.

3. Answer the "Enter range to unprotect" prompt by using the keyboard or mouse to specify a range of cells to mark as unprotected (U).

4. Press ↵ or click the mouse to complete the operation.

● **NOTES**   Use /Range Unprot to turn cell protection off and allow users to make edits or entries. Use this command with /Worksheet Global Protection Enable and /Range Input to control data-entry in fill-in-the-blanks forms. Unprotected cells appear in a different color or with a different intensity. 1-2-3 does not allow you to edit, erase, copy, move, insert or delete rows or columns in a protected worksheet.

Examples

Suppose your worksheet calculates payroll values for hourly employees. Since it contains all employee wage and deduction data, you only need to enter the hours worked. If column F contains HOURS for each employee, you can select **/Worksheet Global Protection Enable** and then **/Range Unprot** for the range F1..F326 representing 325 employees. Unless someone unprotects your other wage cells, no accidental adjustments can occur to the remaining wage data for your employees. To prevent anyone from modifying the wage information, enter a password with the **/File Save** command.

See Also   /Range Input, /Range Prot, and /Worksheet Global.

THE /RANGE VALUE COMMAND

● **PURPOSE**   To copy current values (not formulas) from one range of cells to a new range.

To Make a Value-Only Copy of a Range of Cells:

1. Bring up the Main Menu and select **Range**.

2. Select **Value** from the second-level menu.

3. Answer the "Convert what?" prompt by using the keyboard or mouse to specify a range of cells to consider.

4. Answer the "To where?" prompt by moving the cell pointer to the top-left corner of a destination range.

5. Press ↵ or click the mouse to complete the operation.

● **NOTES**   Formulas in the original conversion range are not copied; only their current values and cell formatting are copied. Press F9 (CALC) if Manual Recalculation mode is active and the formulas must be updated before running the /Range Value command.

Formulas take up more memory than values, so to reduce memory consumption make the destination range in step 4 the top-left corner cell in the conversion range. This rewrites the values in the original cells and replaces the formulas. Do this only if you no longer expect the values to change.

Examples

Suppose your worksheet contains a large database table of all checks written for the entire year. Using the /Data Query Extract command, you have categorized all your expenses for income tax purposes. Placing those individual expense entries in different columns, you have a row of @SUM formulas that add up the individual contributions from all the checks falling into each category.

By the end of the year, the worksheet is fairly large and memory is becoming scarce. You select **/Range Value** and specify the same conversion and destination ranges, so the formulas are replaced in their original cells with their current summation values. Then you erase all the cells containing extracted data from the checkbook database table. These two steps reclaim considerable space for subsequent analysis of your spending habits.

See Also   /Copy, /File Admin, /Range Trans, and @RAND.

THE /SYSTEM COMMAND

● **PURPOSE**   To switch temporarily from 1-2-3 to a DOS command prompt.

To Run DOS Commands:

1. Bring up the Main Menu and select **System**.

2. The 1-2-3 worksheet screen disappears and you see an operating system prompt. Run any sequence of commands or programs.

3. Type **EXIT** and press ↵ to return to your 1-2-3 worksheet.

See Also /Quit

THE TUTOR ADD-IN

● **PURPOSE** To interactively teach how to use the principal features of 1-2-3.

To Learn How to Build a Worksheet:

1. Invoke the TUTOR.

2. Press ↓ to highlight the

Section 1: Building a Worksheet

choice and press ↵.

3. Press ↓ until you've highlighted the subtopic you're interested in:

Overview

Lesson 1: Basic 1-2-3 Skills

Lesson 2: Entering Information in a Worksheet

Lesson 3: Working with Ranges

Lesson 4: Using Formulas

Lesson 5: Linking Files

Lesson 6: Formatting a Worksheet

Lesson 7: Printing a Worksheet

4. Press ↵ to initiate a timed presentation of the selected topic.

This section of the TUTOR concentrates on the fundamentals of worksheets and the parts of a 1-2-3 screen. You will learn about ranges, formats, and formatting.

To Learn How to Create Graphs of Worksheet Data:

1. Invoke the TUTOR and press the **PgDn** key.

2. Press ↓ to highlight the choice below.

Section 2: Using Graphs

3. Press ↓ until you've highlighted the subtopic you're interested in:

Overview

Lesson 8: Creating Graphs

Lesson 9: Working with Several Graphs

4. Press ↵ to initiate a timed presentation of the topic you selected.

This section explains how to both create and print graphs of worksheet data.

To Learn How to Manage a 1-2-3 Database:

1. Invoke the TUTOR and wait for the Table of Contents screen to appear.

2. Press ↓ key to highlight the choice below and then press ↵.

Section 3: Using a Database

3.   Press ↓ until you've highlighted the tutorial subtopics you're interested in:

Overview

Lesson 10: Setting Up and Sorting a Database

Lesson 11: Searching for Information in a Database

4.   Press ↵ to initiate a timed presentation of the selected topic.

To Learn about 1-2-3 Macros:

1.   Invoke the TUTOR and wait for the Table of Contents screen to appear.

2.   Press ↓ to highlight

Section 4: Working with Macros

and press ↵.

3.   Press ↓ until you've highlighted the tutorial subtopic you're interested in:

Overview

Lesson 12: Macro Basics

Lesson 13: Creating Macros with the Learn Feature

Lesson 14: Correcting Errors in Macros

4.   Press ↵ to initiate a timed presentation of the selected topic.

This section explains how to design, write, debug, and execute your macros.

● **NOTES**   You must issue the /Add-In Attach menu choice first to load TUTOR into memory first—only then can you run the program with the /Add-In Invoke command. Alternatively, you can press one of four Alt-function key combinations if you assigned one during the /Add-In Attach process. After you've loaded TUTOR, select Read Me First. To return to your regular 1-2-3 screen, select Quit 1-2-3-Go!

See Also   /Add-In Attach, /Add-In Invoke, AUDITOR, BSOLVER, ICONS, MACROMGR, VIEWER, and WYSIWYG.

THE VIEWER ADD-IN

● **PURPOSE**   To view the contents of disk-based worksheets quickly during other 1-2-3 operations.

To View and Retrieve a Worksheet on Disk:

1. Run the VIEWER and select **Retrieve**.

2. 1-2-3 prompts you to save your work if your current worksheet contains changes that have not yet been saved. To discard your changes, select **Yes**—the Viewer will continue the Retrieve procedure. To return to Ready mode, select **No**.

3. Press ↓ to highlight the names of worksheets found in the current directory. When a worksheet name is highlighted, the VIEWER displays the top-left corner range of cells in the VIEW window on the right side of the screen.

4. Press the ← to display a list of any worksheet names in the current directory's parent. If you are highlighting a directory name, press → to display a list of worksheet and directory names in the next lower position in the directory tree.

5. If you are viewing a worksheet entry, press → to move the cell pointer into the VIEW window. Now you can use cell pointer movement keys to view any cells in the worksheet. To return to the worksheet name list, press **Home** and ←.

6. Press ↵ to retrieve the currently highlighted worksheet.

Use **Retrieve** to peek at the contents of a worksheet before you load it into memory. After you've selected Retrieve, press F5 to display file names by date (most recent ones first) or F6 to display names alphabetically. After you've changed directories, press **F2** to reset to the original current directory.

To Enter a Linking Formula:

1. Move the cell pointer to the cell where you want to write the linking formula. See the "Notes" section below to find out how to ask the VIEWER to automatically write a group of linking formulas.

2. Run the VIEWER and select **Link**.

3. Press ↓ to highlight the names of worksheets found in the current directory. When a subdirectory name is highlighted, the VIEWER displays a list of worksheet files on the right side of the screen. When a worksheet name is highlighted, the VIEWER displays the top-left corner range of cells in the VIEW window on the right side of the screen.

4. Press ← to display a list of worksheet names in the current directory's parent. If you are highlighting a directory name, press → to display a list of worksheet and directory names in the next lower position in the directory tree.

5. If you are viewing a worksheet entry, press → to move the cell pointer into the VIEW window. Now you can use cell pointer movement keys to view any cells in the worksheet. To return to the worksheet name list, press **Home**-←.

6. You can ask the VIEWER to write one or more formulas in the cell or cells to link them to the currently viewed cell or highlighted cell range of a disk worksheet:

a. Press → and then ↵ to link to the single cell containing the cell pointer in the VIEW window.

b. Anchor the range by pressing the period key or by double-clicking the mouse—that is pressing the mouse button twice in rapid succession. Highlight a larger range with the cursor keys or by clicking the mouse on an opposite corner of the range. Press ↵ to write a block of linking formulas in the original worksheet that link to each of the cells highlighted in the VIEW window.

7. If the original worksheet cells contain data, VIEWER warns you that it will overwrite these non-blank cells with the newly constructed linking formulas. Select **Yes** to allow the overwriting, or **No** to return to the linking mode screen of the VIEWER. You can then press **Esc** several times to return to Ready mode.

To Display the Contents of Worksheet Files on Disk:

1. Run the VIEWER and select **Browse**.

2. Press ↓ to highlight each file name found in the current directory. When a file name is highlighted, the VIEWER displays the top few lines (of non-worksheet files) or the left-corner range of cells (of worksheets) in the VIEW window on the right side of the screen.

3. Press ← to display a list of existing file names in the current directory's parent. If you are highlighting a directory name, press → to display a list of file and directory names in that next lower position in the directory tree.

4. If you are viewing a file entry, press → to move the highlighting into the VIEW window. For worksheets, use the cell pointer movement keys to view any cells in the worksheet. For non-worksheets, press ↑ and ↓ to view the contents.

5. Return to the file name list by pressing **Home-←**.

6. Press ↵ to return to Ready mode.

● **NOTES**   You must use the / Add-In Attach menu choice first to load the VIEWER into memory. Run the program with the / Add-In Invoke command or by pressing one of four Alt-function key combinations, provided you made an Alt-function key assignment during the / Add-In Attach process.

Examples

Suppose you are constructing a consolidation worksheet to add up the submitted contributions to revenue from four different subsidiaries. You write a formula @SUM(D1..D4), planning to link cells D1..D4 to each of the four submitted revenue worksheets (named SUB1, SUB2, SUB3, and SUB4) submitted by each subsidiary's general manager. Since you sent the original worksheet skeleton to each manager, you know that the necessary final dollar value in each worksheet can be found in cell X25.

First, move the cell pointer to cell D1, run the VIEWER, and select **Link**. Move the highlight down to worksheet name SUB1.WK1, and press → to move into the VIEW window. Move the cell pointer to cell X25 and press ↵. The VIEWER writes a formula into cell D1 that links that cell to the X25 cell of the SUB1 worksheet:

+<<C:\123R23\SUB1.WK1>>X25

Repeat this process for the other three cells (D2, D3, and D4), linking them to the respective X25 cells in worksheets SUB2, SUB3, and SUB4.

See Also   / Add-In Attach, / Add-In Invoke, AUDITOR, BSOLVER, ICONS, /File Admin, /FileView, MACROMGR, TUTOR, and WYSIWYG.

THE /WORKSHEET COLUMN COMMAND

● **PURPOSE**   To adjust the width of a column, or to hide a column.

To Initiate the /Worksheet Column Command:

1. Bring up the Main Menu and select **Worksheet**.

2. Select **Column** from the second-level menu. A third level menu appears with the following choices:

Set-Width—Adjusts the current column's width.

Reset-Width—Sets the current column's width to the global column width.

Hide—Hides a column range from view.

Display—Redisplays hidden columns.

Column-Range—Adjusts the width of multiple columns at the same time.

When you widen or shrink a column, 1-2-3 will ask you to type a new number of characters to represent the width. Alternatively you can press → or ← to change the column width. Press ↵ to complete the operation.

When you hide or redisplay hidden columns, use the keyboard or mouse to specify the columns to hide or redisplay (after you've chosen Hide or Display). Press ↵ to complete the operation.

To Widen, Shrink, or Reset the Width of Several Columns:

1. Select **Set-Width** or **Reset-Width** from the Column-Range submenu.

2. Use the keyboard or mouse to define the range of columns to be affected.

3. Type a new width or use the arrow keys to change the width of all columns at once.

4. Press ↵ or click the mouse to complete the operation.

● **NOTES**   Hide columns to prevent others from seeing the data onscreen or in printouts. Also, use this command to suppress intervening columns and thereby print non-adjacent columns together.

Examples

Suppose your personnel worksheet contains employee names and wages. To reduce the likelihood of snooping, you decide to suppress the display of column G, which contains each employee's weekly wage. To do so, move the cell pointer to any cell in column G and select **/Worksheet Column Hide**. In the column headings, you now see column F followed by column H.

See Also   /Range Search, /Worksheet Global, and /Worksheet Window.

THE /WORKSHEET DELETE COMMAND

● **PURPOSE**   To completely remove columns or rows and their contents from a worksheet.

To Delete Worksheet Rows or Columns:

1.   Bring up the Main Menu and select **Worksheet**.

2.   Select **Delete** from the second-level menu.

3.   Select **Column** (or **Row**) to delete one or more columns (or rows).

4.   Answer the "Enter range of columns (or rows) to delete" prompt by using the keyboard or mouse to extend the highlight to span all the columns (or rows) you want to remove from your worksheet.

5.   Press ⏎ or click the mouse to complete the operation.

● **NOTES**   If any rows or columns are hidden, they are temporarily redisplayed with an asterisk beside the column letter during this deletion operation.

Examples

Suppose one of your customers has gone out of business. Since you use your customer database to send out regular promotional literature, you must remove that customer's entry from the worksheet. First, move the cell pointer to the row containing the customer's information. Then, select **/Worksheet Delete Row**. Since you are only removing this one row, press ↵ to delete the entire row.

See Also   /File Erase, /Range Erase, /Worksheet Insert, and /Worksheet Page.

THE /WORKSHEET ERASE COMMAND

● **PURPOSE**   To erase the entire current worksheet and be able to begin a new worksheet from scratch.

To Clear All Worksheet Information from Memory:

1.   Bring up the Main Menu and select **Worksheet**.

2.   Select **Erase** from the second-level menu.

3.   Select **Yes** if you want 1-2-3 to erase all worksheet data from memory; or **No** to return to Ready mode and avoid accidentally erasing the worksheet.

4.   1-2-3 will tell you if worksheet changes have not yet been saved. Select **Yes** to erase the worksheet at this time and discard the unsaved changes, or **No** to return to Ready mode.

• **NOTES** This command does not affect the disk copy of the worksheet. Use this command to erase the memory area used for worksheets when you are ready to begin working on a new worksheet.

Examples

Suppose you have spent thirty minutes balancing your checkbook with the appropriate worksheet. Now, after saving your checkbook worksheet, you are ready to begin the design of a totally new worksheet for analyzing investments. Select **/Worksheet Erase**, and respond with **Yes**.

See Also /File Erase, /Range Erase, and /Worksheet Delete.

THE /WORKSHEET GLOBAL COMMAND

• **PURPOSE** To specify 1-2-3's configuration settings for both the entire work session and for the current worksheet.

To Initiate the /Worksheet Global Command:

1. Bring up the Main Menu and select **Worksheet**.

2. Select **Global** from the second-level menu.

3. From the third-level menu, select one of the following choices:

Format—Sets the default appearance of data. (See /Range Format for an explanation of all display formats.)

Label-Prefix—Sets the default alignment of labels. (See /Range Label for an explanation of all alignment types.)

Column-Width—Sets the default width of columns. (See /Worksheet Column for width adjustment possibilities.)

Recalculation—Sets the sequence and way in which cell formulas that depend on other cells are computed.

Protection—Toggles overall worksheet protection on or off.

Default—Sets the default 1-2-3 configuration values for the printer, clock formats, expanded memory use, and so on.

Zero—Controls how numeric zero values appear.

If you select Recalculation in step 3, you will see another submenu:

- **Natural** computes formulas in the normal order of cell dependencies.

- **Columnwise** or **Rowwise** force calculation column by column, or row by row.

- **Automatic** forces recalculation of all formulas whenever any cell entries are made.

- **Manual** specifies recalculation only when you press F9 (or execute the CALC macro instruction).

- **Iteration** controls how many recalculation passes are performed if your worksheet contains circular references, or if you've previously selected Columnwise or Rowwise calculation.

If you select Default in step 3 above, you will see another submenu:

- **Printer** specifies interface and initial printed output default values.

- **Directory** defines the assumed disk directory for /File commands.

- **Status** temporarily displays a window containing all 1-2-3 default settings.

- **Update** stores all current default settings in a .CNF configuration file.

- **Other** sets a miscellany of default values, including status line information, UNDO activation, expanded memory use, Add-In usage, and the appearance of international data.

- **Autoexec** toggles on or off the execution of a macro named \0 (if it exists) when you retrieve a worksheet.

/Global menu choices result in settings that apply to all cells in the current worksheet. However, these global settings can be overridden by individual adjustments from other 1-2-3 commands (most often a /Range command).

Examples

Suppose your office has a calendar and you have a watch, so viewing the date and time on the status line is not helpful. However, you sometimes are not sure which worksheet you are working on, so viewing the filename would be very useful. Select **/Worksheet Global Default Other Clock Filename Update Quit**. You will now see the worksheet file name you are using whenever you retrieve a worksheet.

See Also   /File Directory, /Print Encoded, /Print Printer, /Range Erase, /Range Format, /Range Input, /Range Justify, /Range Label, /Range Prot, /Range Unprot, /Worksheet Column, /Worksheet Erase, /Worksheet Status, /Worksheet Window, and @INT.

THE /WORKSHEET INSERT COMMAND

- **PURPOSE**   To add new rows or columns to a worksheet.

To Insert Blank Columns or Rows:

1. Bring up the Main Menu and select **Worksheet**.

2. Select **Insert** from the second-level menu.

3. Select **Column** (or **Row**) to include one or more columns (or rows) to the left (or just above) the location of the cell pointer.

4. Answer the "Enter column (or row) insert range" prompt by using the keyboard or mouse to extend the highlight to span the number of columns (or rows) you want to add to the worksheet.

5. Press ↵ or click the mouse to complete the operation.

● **NOTES**   Existing columns (or rows) are moved to the right (or down) to make room for the newly created cells. Both data contents and formatting are moved. The newly inserted cells are completely blank. You will probably have to reformat these cells before successfully entering new data that appears correct.

Examples

Let's say you had a terrific day on the phone, developing five new customer contacts. To add five new entries to your customer worksheet, move the cell pointer to the row where you want to enter all five new customers. Select **/Worksheet Insert Row** and extend the cell highlight to span five rows. Press ↵ or click the mouse to open up five new blank rows in which to type the new customer data.

See Also   /Worksheet Delete

THE /WORKSHEET LEARN COMMAND

● **PURPOSE**   To capture keystrokes for the purpose of automating the creation of 1-2-3 macros.

To Set, Cancel, or Erase the Learn Range:

1. Bring up the Main Menu and select **Worksheet**.

2. Select **Learn** from the second-level menu.

3. A third-level menu appears from which you must select one of three choices:

Range—Specifies a one-column group of cells to record keystrokes when Learn mode is on (after pressing Alt-F5).

Cancel—Disassociates the current Learn range from the keystroke recording process.

Erase—Clears out any recorded keystrokes from the current Learn range.

● **NOTES** If the Learn range fills up during automatic recording, you can choose /Worksheet Learn Range once again to enlarge the range and continue recording keystrokes. Use the Cancel choice to retain recorded keystrokes in the former Learn range, and then define a new range to capture future keystrokes for a new macro. Use the Erase choice to retain the current Learn range, but erase all captured keystrokes so you can begin a new macro sequence from scratch.

Examples

Suppose that you intend to produce a weekly printout of all customers purchasing more than $2000 from your equipment warehouse. To do this, you plan to write a macro that automatically performs a **/Data Query Extract** of the appropriate data and prints the information.

First, you call up the SALES worksheet and define the Learn range by selecting **/Worksheet Learn Range**. You move the cell pointer to cell F10, anchor the range, and extend the highlight to cell F40 to complete the definition of the Learn range. You press **Alt-F5** to turn on Learn mode. Assuming—since they won't change from week to week—that you've previously specified the Input, Criteria, and Output ranges from the /Data Query menu, you can now capture just the keystrokes necessary to extract and print the selected data.

Select **/Data Query Extract Quit**. The extracted data appears in the Output range. Select **/Print Printer Range** and specify the range you think will include the expected data rows, say A16..D46, assuming you have no more than 30 big-ticket customers in one week. Next press ⏎ and select **Align Go Page Quit** to complete the captured macro instructions. Turn Learn mode off, move the cell pointer to cell E10, and type **WEEKLY**, the name of this macro. You will observe the following keystrokes that 1-2-3 captures and stores in the Learn range (beginning with F10):

/dqeq

/ppra16..d46agpq

Select **/Range Name Create** and assign the name WEEKLY to cell F10, the beginning of the Learn range and now also the beginning of the WEEKLY macro. To run this macro quickly, press **Alt-F3** and select WEEKLY from the list of macros that appears. The data extraction occurs, depositing the results in the output range, and the macro then prints the extracted rows and quits.

THE /WORKSHEET PAGE COMMAND

- **PURPOSE**   To control pagination during printing.

To Insert a Page Break Code into Your Worksheet:

1.   Bring up the Main Menu and select **Worksheet**.

2.   Select **Page** from the second-level menu.

- **NOTES**   This command inserts a page break code (::) in the current cell and moves all worksheet rows down by one to make room for the code.

See Also   /Range Erase and /Worksheet Delete.

THE /WORKSHEET STATUS COMMAND

● **PURPOSE**   To display information about system memory and other hardware, as well as circular formula references that may exist in the current worksheet.

To Display a Screen Window Containing Worksheet Status Information:

1.   Bring up the Main Menu and select **Worksheet**.

2.   Select **Status** from the second-level menu.

● **NOTES**   This screen lists information about memory use, circular references, and math co-processor existence. To view global settings, use the /Worksheet Global command. To view configuration settings, use the /Worksheet Global Default Status command.

See Also   /Worksheet Global.

THE /WORKSHEET TITLES COMMAND

● **PURPOSE**   To create unmoving column headings or row names for both on-screen viewing and printouts.

To Prevent the Scrolling of Rows or Columns on the Screen:

1.   Bring up the Main Menu and select **Worksheet**.

2. Select **Titles** from the second-level menu.

3. A third-level menu appears from which you must select one choice:

> **Both**—Locks onscreen all rows above the current one, and all columns to the left of the current one.
>
> **Horizontal**—Locks onscreen all rows above the current one.
>
> **Vertical**—Locks onscreen all columns to the left of the current one.
>
> **Clear**—Unlocks all frozen columns or rows, permitting you to scroll once again through formerly locked data.

● **NOTES**   Use this command in very long or wide worksheets as a means of retaining important titles or labels onscreen as you scroll through many similar rows or columns of data.

Examples

Suppose your inventory worksheet contains information for thousands of parts, with the database table headings row appearing only once in row one. Move the cell pointer to row 2 and select **/Worksheet Titles Horizontal**. Now you can move to any inventory item row and still view the important column headings.

See Also   /Worksheet Window

THE /WORKSHEET WINDOW COMMAND

● **PURPOSE**   To split the screen into two windows and view separate portions of the current worksheet simultaneously.

To Split the Screen Display
into Two Horizontal or Vertical Windows:

1. Move the cell pointer to any cell in the row or column at which you want to split the screen.

2. Bring up the Main Menu and select **Worksheet**.

3. Select **Window** from the second-level menu.

4. A third-level menu appears from which you must make one choice:

Horizontal—Creates two screen windows, both of which you can scroll through, with an extra set of column identifiers inserted just above the current row.

Vertical—Creates two screen windows, both of which you can scroll through, with an extra set of row identifiers inserted just to the left of the current column.

Sync—Allows you to scroll through horizontal or vertical windows and have the same columns or rows scroll simultaneously in both windows.

Unsync—Removes window synchronization so that cell pointer movement in one window has no effect on the display in the other window.

Clear—Returns the screen to a single window display and enlarges either the left or top window to full screen size.

Press F6 to move the cell pointer between the two windows.

● **NOTES**   The Horizontal and Vertical options control whether one or two windows appear on your screen, while the Sync and Unsync choices control the parallel movement between row and column display in the two windows. Use the /Worksheet Titles command in conjunction with /Worksheet Window to lock certain labels in each screen window. This makes it easier to view and identify the data in each window.

Examples

Suppose your worksheet contains both outstanding invoices as well as newly posted payments. They exist in two separate ranges: A1..F100 contains payments, and A201..F300 contain invoices. In order to view related entries in both ranges, you move the cell pointer to cell A201, make sure it is located roughly in the middle of the screen, and select **/Worksheet Window Horizontal**. Now, to make entries or edits in either the invoice or payment groups, all you have to do is press **F6** to switch back and forth between the windows.

See Also   /Worksheet Column, /Worksheet Global, and /Worksheet Titles.

THE WYSIWYG ADD-IN

● **PURPOSE**   To enhance the screen and printed versions of your worksheets by augmenting standard 1-2-3 features with new facilities for controlling graphics and fonts. (This Add-In is only available in Version 2.3.)

To Control Worksheet
Rows, Columns, and Pagination:

1. Select **Worksheet** from the WYSIWYG Main Menu.

2. Select **Column**, **Row**, or **Page** from the submenu that appears:

   Column—Adjusts the width of one or more adjacent columns. After you've made this selection, choose **Set-Width** to widen or shrink column width; or **Reset-Width** to restore column width to the global value. In either case, answer the "Select the columns to set width to" prompt by specifying one or more columns to be affected. Press ↵ or click the mouse to complete the operation.

   Row—Adjusts the height of one or more adjacent rows. After you've made this selection, choose **Set-Height** to specify the row height yourself; or **Auto** to allow WYSIWYG to set row height according to the largest font you are using in the row. If you choose **Set-Height**, you must answer the "new row height in points (1..255)" prompt by typing a number and pressing ↵ to complete the operation. Whether you choose **Auto** or **Set-Height**, answer the "Select the rows to set height to" prompt by specifying one or more rows to be affected. Press ↵ or click the mouse.

Page—Inserts or deletes page breaks between rows and columns. After you've made this selection, choose **Row** to insert a page break—an indicator that begins a new page—when printing the current row; **Column** to insert a page break when printing the current column; or **Delete** to remove any previously inserted page breaks at the current row and column.

Column width adjustments remain in effect, even after WYSIWYG is removed from memory. Row height adjustments, on the other hand, are discarded if WYSIWYG is removed from memory.

To Control Overall Worksheet Appearance:

1. Select **Format** from the WYSIWYG Main Menu.

2. Select one choice from the submenu that appears and answer any prompts that follow:

Font—Displays a submenu that controls fonts. Options **1** to **8** allow you to apply one of up to eight fonts to a cell range. **Replace** changes one of the eight fonts with another font. **Default** uses the default font set or creates a new group of eight fonts. **Library** saves, retrieves, or deletes a disk-based font library.

Bold—Displays a submenu for controlling boldface text. **Set** makes the data in a range boldface. **Clear** removes boldface from the data in a range. Answer the "Change the attributes of range" prompt by specifying the range of cells to affect.

Italics—Displays a submenu for controlling italic text. **Set** italicizes the data in a range. **Clear** removes italics from the data in a range. Answer the "Change the attributes of range" prompt by specifying the range of cells to affect.

Underline—Displays a submenu for controlling underlining. **Single** underlines the non-blank data in a range. **Double** draws a pair of lines under the non-blank data in a range. **Wide** draws a thick line under the non-blank data in a range. Answer the "Change the attributes of range" prompt by specifying the range of cells to affect.

Color—Displays a submenu for controlling color. **Text** allows you to choose one of seven colors for displaying characters in a range. **Background** is for choosing the screen background color. **Negative** lets you choose a color for negative numbers in a range. **Reverse** switches the colors of the background and characters in a range.

Lines—Displays a series of submenus to specify shadows behind a range, or single, double, or wide lines on one to four sides of a range or on the cells within a range.

Shade—Displays a submenu for controlling shading. **Clear**, **Light**, **Dark**, and **Solid** add zero, low, medium, and heavy shading, respectively, to a range of cells.

Reset—Removes all formatting and named-style adjustments to a range of cells.

To Manage Worksheet Graphics:

1. Select **Graph** from the WYSIWYG Main Menu.

2. Select one choice from the submenu that appears and answer any prompts that follow:

Add—Places a graphic entry in the worksheet. The entry can be the current graph, a named graph, a stored .PIC file, a .CGM metafile, or simply a placeholder for a future graphic entry.

Remove—Removes a specified graphic entry in a worksheet. Underlying data or stored graphic information is not affected.

Goto—Moves the cell pointer directly to one of the worksheet's graphic entries.

Settings—Controls a variety of graph settings by way of the submenu that appears. **Graph** controls individual graphic entries; **Range** the location *and* size of an entry; **Sync** the automatic or manual updating mode; **Display** the non-display of selected graphics; and **Opaque** the resolution of worksheet data underlying a graphic entry.

Move—Relocates, without resizing, a graphic entry.

Zoom—Displays a full-screen version of any graphic entry temporarily.

Compute—Recalculates and updates all graphic entries in your WYSIWYG worksheet.

View—Displays a full-screen version of any .PIC or .CGM graphic file temporarily.

Edit—Makes adjustments to any graphic entry by way of a submenu. **Add** places additional information on a graph. **Select** specifies one or more objects to be edited. **Edit** changes individual object appearance. **Color** specifies colors for part or all of a graphic entry. **Transform** changes size or orientation. **Rearrange** modifies the location, existence, and availability of all objects in the graphic. **View** adjusts the size of the graphics editing window. **Options** controls grid lines, text size, and cursor size.

To Print All WYSIWYG Data, Fonts, and Graphics:

1. Select **Print** from the WYSIWYG Main Menu.

2. Select one choice from the submenu that appears and answer any prompts that follow:

Go—Prints the selected and formatted range.

File—Prints to a .ENC disk file encoded for later printing to the current printer.

Background—Prints to a .ENC disk file encoded for the current system printer, and used immediately for printing while you initiate other worksheet operations.

Range—Sets or clears the block or blocks of cells to be printed. Use semicolons (;) to separate multiple print ranges, and include spillover cells when printing long labels.

Config—Configures printing instructions by providing a submenu. **Printer** allows you to specify a printer; **Interface** to select the port for print output; **1st-Cart** or **2nd-Cart** to choose which font cartridge to use; **Orientation** to specify landscape or portrait printing; and **Bin** to indicate which paper feed operation to use. You must select a graphics printer driver with the Config choice before WYSIWYG will print any worksheet data at all.

Settings—Defines the print settings for the WYSIWYG session. **Begin** and **End** identify the first and last page number to print. **Start** assigns the beginning page number. **Copies** indicates how many automatic printouts to produce of the specified range. **Wait** pauses after printing each page. **Grid** specifies whether the grid prints along with the range. **Frame** specifies whether or not the worksheet frame prints along with the range. **Reset** restores all original WYSIWYG settings.

Layout—Defines the page appearance and positioning. **Page-Size** sets the length and width. **Margins** sets any or all of the four page margins. **Titles** defines headers or footers. **Borders** sets or clears border ranges to print. **Compression** shrinks or expands a print range when printing. **Default** restores or permanently adjusts the default WYSIWYG page layout settings. **Library** saves, restores, or erases .LBR files that contain WYSIWYG page layouts.

Preview—Displays the print range temporarily, page by page.

Info—Toggles between showing and suppressing the WYSIWYG Print Settings window.

To Control Video Monitor Characteristics:

1. Select **Display** from the WYSIWYG Main Menu.

2. Select one choice from the submenu that appears and answer any prompts that follow:

Mode—Establishes graphics or text display resolution, and sets color displays on or off.

Zoom—Shrinks or enlarges the on-screen size of cell data.

Colors—Sets the on-screen default colors for portions of the screen and types of data and cells.

Options—Sets a variety of visual effects on such elements as frames, grids, cell pointers, and page breaks.

Font-Directory—Sets the directory containing the WYSIWYG fonts.

Rows—Specifies how many screen rows are to appear.

Default—Restores or permanently adjusts the default WYSIWYG display settings.

To Manage WYSIWYG Cell Formatting:

1. Select **Special** from the WYSIWYG Main Menu.

2. Select one choice from the submenu that appears and answer any prompts that follow:

Copy—Replicates a range's formatting at another worksheet location.

Move—Relocates a range's formats to another worksheet range.

Import—Reads and applies the formatting of a WYSIWYG, Impress, or Allways file to the current worksheet data.

Export—Stores current formatting in a WYSIWYG, Impress, or Allways format file.

To Manipulate WYSIWYG Text Labels:

1. Select **Text** from the WYSIWYG Main Menu.

2. Select one choice from the submenu that appears and answer any prompts that follow:

Edit—Enters or modifies labels in worksheet cells.

Align—Positions labels with respect to the center of a range, or the left and right edges.

Reformat—Justifies the first column of text range labels to fit within the range specified.

Set—Specifies a range in which to use the Text commands.

Clear—Removes the text formatting from a range of cells.

To Define or Apply a Named Style:

1. Select **Named-Style** from the WYSIWYG Main Menu.

2. A submenu appears with the options 1 through 8 and a final option, Define.

    a. To apply an existing style to a range, select one of eight listed style choices. Answer the "Change the attributes of range" prompt by using the keyboard or mouse to tell 1-2-3 the cells to apply the specified style to.

    b. To define a new style, or redefine one of the existing eight styles, choose Define and select one of the eight choices that appear. Specify which cell's formatting style to use, and type a name and description for the style.

● **NOTES** You must first use the /Add-In Attach menu choice to load WYSIWYG into memory. This program is automatically activated. To bring up its own special menu line, press the colon (:) key. Pressing the colon key is quicker then running the WYSIWYG program with the /Add-In Invoke command or with an Alt-function key combination you assign.

Examples

Suppose your worksheet contains a database table in A1..D40 and a computed summary graph to the right of the table in cells G6..K12. To use WYSIWYG to print both tables in one easy request, but on separate pieces of paper, move the cell pointer to the first column of the right side table. Next, bring up WYSIWYG by pressing the colon (:) key, and insert a vertical page break by selecting **Worksheet Page Column**. Next, bring up the WYSIWYG **:Print** menu and specify the range to print, A1..K40 in this case to span both intended print pages. If you haven't done it previously, remember to first select a graphic printer driver with the **:Print Config Printer** option.

See Also /Add-In Attach, /Add-In Invoke, AUDITOR, BSOLVER, ICONS, MACROMGR, TUTOR, and VIEWER.

Part III

Using the 1-2-3 Functions

In this Part, you can quickly look up the syntax of any 1-2-3 function. The entries are arranged alphabetically and each includes a definition of the function's purpose and practical examples of how and when to use it. The entries include special recommendations for using each function effectively.

1-2-3 groups its functions into nine categories:

Add-In	Used to expand the number of @ functions available (through Add-In programs) for processing 1-2-3 cell data.
Database	Used to perform database table analyses and queries.
Date and Time	Used to manipulate values that represent dates and times.
Financial	Used to compute loans, annuities, and cash-flow factors.
Logical	Used to compute conditional values or formulas.
Mathematical	Used to compute common scientific, algebraic, and trigonometric formula operations.
Special	Used to perform a number of unique or special-purpose chores.
Statistical	Used to compute formulas applied to a list or group of values.
String	Used to manipulate labels and string expressions.

Table III.1 summarizes all of 1-2-3's functions by categories of application.

Table III.1: 1-2-3 Functions by Category

Category	Function
Database	@DAVG, @DCOUNT, @DMAX, @DMIN, @DSTD, @DSUM, @DVAR.
Date and Time	@DATE, @DATEVALUE, @DAY, @HOUR, @MINUTE, @MONTH, @NOW, @SECOND, @TIME, @TIMEVALUE, @YEAR.
Financial	@CTERM, @DDB, @FV, @IRR, @NPV, @PMT, @PV, @RATE, @SLN, @SYD, @TERM.
Logical	@FALSE, @IF, @ISAAF, @ISAPP, @ISERR, @ISNA, @ISNUMBER, @ISSTRING, @TRUE.
Mathematical	@ABS, @ACOS, @ASIN, @ATAN, @ATAN2, @COS, @EXP, @INT, @LN, @LOG, @MOD, @PI, @RAND, @ROUND, @SIN, @SQRT, @TAN.
Special	@@, @?, @CELL, @CELLPOINTER, @CHOOSE, @COLS, @ERR, @HLOOKUP, @INDEX, @NA, @ROWS, @VLOOKUP.
Statistical	@AVG, @COUNT, @MAX, @MIN, @STD, @SUM, @VAR.
String	@CHAR, @CLEAN, @CODE, @EXACT, @FIND, @LEFT, @LENGTH, @LOWER, @MID, @N, @PROPER, @REPEAT, @REPLACE, @RIGHT, @S, @STRING, @TRIM, @UPPER, @VALUE.

@?

- **PURPOSE**   To call attention to an unidentified function.

- **SYNTAX**

  @?

- **NOTES**   You can't enter this function into a cell. Because 1-2-3 allows you to incorporate @ functions specific to certain Add-Ins in your worksheet, it is possible for a worksheet to be retrieved before the referenced Add-In has been attached. When this happens, the @ function that the worksheet references is unknown, 1-2-3 replaces it with @?, and the resulting value is NA. Remember to attach Add-Ins before you retrieve worksheets that use specialized functions from the Add-In.

See Also   / Add-In Attach, and these other special functions: @@, @CELL, @CELLPOINTER, @CHOOSE, @COLS, @ERR, @HLOOKUP, @INDEX, @NA, @ROWS, and @VLOOKUP.

@@

- **PURPOSE**   To provide indirect access for cell referencing.

- **SYNTAX**

  @@(*Address*)

where *Address* is a cell reference. The @@ function returns the cell contents found at *Address*.

- **NOTES**   The cell reference *Address* can be a direct cell address, such as A5 or a range name, or a formula such as @IF, which results in a label that is a cell address.

Examples

Suppose that cell B1 contained the label "D6", and cell D6 contained the value .35 (or 35%). If cell B2 contained the formula

@@(B1) * 100

it would evaluate first to .35 * 100, or 35. Furthermore, suppose cell E2 contained an employee's annual salary (50,000), and cells D4..D6 contained a small table of tax rates—15%, 25%, 35%. Cell B1 could use an @IF function to determine which tax rate to use in calculating how much total tax is owed:

@IF(E2<50000,"D4",@IF(E2<100000,"D5","D6"))

This results in cell B1 containing

- the label "D4" if the salary in E2 is less than 50,000;

- the label "D5" if the salary is at least 50,000 but less than 100,000; or

- the label "D6" if the salary is 100,000 or more.

Cell B2 could compute total taxes owed by using a formula that multiplies the tax rate—found indirectly through cell B1, in one of the D4..D6 entries—by the salary in E2:

+E2 * @@(B1)

In this example, the formula would result in

+E2 * D5, or

+50000 * .25, or

12,500

Remember to start the formula with a plus sign to keep 1-2-3 from accidentally treating your formula as a label that begins with the letter *E*.

See Also   These other functions: @?, @CELL, @CELLPOINTER, @CHOOSE, @COLS, @ERR, @HLOOKUP, @INDEX, @NA, @ROWS, and @VLOOKUP.

@ABS

- **PURPOSE**   To compute the absolute value of a numeric expression.

- **SYNTAX**

    @ABS(*x*)

where *x* is any numeric value.

- **NOTES**   Computing an absolute value always changes negative quantities into positive ones.

Examples

The expression @ABS(–23) results in the positive quantity 23. If cell B7 contains –294, then @ABS(B7) results in the positive quantity 294.

See Also   These other mathematical functions: @ACOS, @ASIN, @ATAN, @ATAN2, @COS, @EXP, @INT, @LN, @LOG, @MOD, @PI, @RAND, @ROUND, @SIN, @SQRT, and @TAN.

@ACOS

- **PURPOSE**   To calculate an angle in radians, such as the arc cosine, given the cosine of the angle.

- **SYNTAX**

    @ACOS(*x*)

where *x* is a value representing the desired angle's cosine.

• **NOTES** The value of x can range from –1 to +1. Remember that there are 2 π radians in 360 degrees. You can convert the resulting angle in radians to degrees by using the @PI function

Angle in Degrees = 180/@PI * Angle in Radians

The @ACOS function will return an angle between 0 and π radians.

Examples

If cell B1 contained 0.5, then @ACOS(B1) would equal 1.047197 radians. Multiplying that value by 180 and dividing by the constant function @PI would result in a value of 60 degrees.

If cell C1 contained 0.866025, then @ACOS(C1) would equal 0.523599 radians. Multiplying that value by 180 and dividing by the constant function @PI would result in a value of 30 degrees.

See Also These other mathematical functions: @ABS, @ASIN, @ATAN, @ATAN2, @COS, @EXP, @INT, @LN, @LOG, @MOD, @PI, @RAND, @ROUND, @SIN, @SQRT, and @TAN.

@ASIN

• **PURPOSE** To calculate an angle in radians, such as the arc sine, given the sine of the angle.

• **SYNTAX**

@ASIN(*x*)

where x is a value representing the desired angle's sine.

• **NOTES** The value of x can range from –1 to +1. Remember that there are 2 π radians in 360 degrees. You can convert to degrees the resulting angle in radians by using the @PI function

Angle in Degrees = 180/@PI * Angle in Radians

The @ASIN function will return an angle between $-\pi/2$ and $+\pi/2$ radians.

Examples

If cell B1 contained 0.5, then @ASIN(B1) would equal 0.523598 radians. Multiplying that value by 180 and dividing by the constant function @PI would result in a value of 30 degrees.

If cell C1 contained 0.866025, then @ASIN(C1) would equal 1.047195512 radians. Multiplying that value by 180 and dividing by the constant function @PI would result in a value of 60 degrees.

See Also   These other mathematical functions: @ABS, @ACOS, @ATAN, @ATAN2, @COS, @EXP, @INT, @LN, @LOG, @MOD, @PI, @RAND, @ROUND, @SIN, @SQRT, and @TAN.

@ATAN

● **PURPOSE**   To calculate an angle in radians, such as the arc tangent, given the tangent of the angle.

● **SYNTAX**

@ATAN(*x*)

where *x* is a value representing the desired angle's tangent.

● **NOTES** X can have any value. Remember that there are 2π radians in 360 degrees. You can convert to degrees the resulting angle in radians by using the @PI function

Angle in Degrees = 180/@PI * Angle in Radians

The @ATAN function returns an angle between $-\pi/2$ and $+\pi/2$ radians.

Examples

If cell B1 contained 1.0, then @ATAN(B1) would equal 0.785398 radians. Multiplying that value by 180 and dividing by the constant function @PI would result in a value of 45 degrees.

See Also   These other mathematical functions: @ABS, @ACOS, @ASIN, @ATAN2, @COS, @EXP, @INT, @LN, @LOG, @MOD, @PI, @RAND, @ROUND, @SIN, @SQRT, and @TAN.

@ATAN2

• **PURPOSE**   To calculate the four quadrant angles in radians, such as the arc tangent, given the two value Y/X tangent of the angle.

• **SYNTAX**

@ATAN2(x,y)

where

- • x is a value representing the desired angle's x-axis side, and

- • y is a value representing the desired angle's y-axis side.

• **NOTES**   X and y can have any value. Remember that there are 2 π radians in 360 degrees. You can convert the resulting angle in radians to degrees by using the @PI function

Angle in Degrees = 180/@PI * Angle in Radians

The @ATAN2 function returns an angle between $-\pi$ and $+\pi$ radians. If x and y are both equal to zero, then @ATAN2 returns a value of ERR.

Examples

If x equaled −1.73205, the negative square root of 3, and y equaled 1.0, then @ATAN2(x,y) would equal 2.617993 radians. Multiplying that value by 180 and dividing by the constant function @PI would result in a value of 150 degrees.

If x equaled 0 and y equaled 1.0, then @ATAN2(x,y) would equal 1.570796 radians. Multiplying that value by 180 and dividing by the constant function @PI would result in a value of 90 degrees.

See Also   These other mathematical functions: @ABS, @ACOS, @ASIN, @ATAN, @COS, @EXP, @INT, @LN, @LOG, @MOD, @PI, @RAND, @ROUND, @SIN, @SQRT, and @TAN.

@AVG

● **PURPOSE**   To calculate the statistical average, also called the *mean value,* of a group of 1-2-3 cells.

● **SYNTAX**

   @AVG(*list*)

where *list* is any series of 1-2-3 cells or range names separated by commas.

● **NOTES**   When you calculate statistical averages, be careful which cell names and ranges you include in your *list*. Statistical functions attempt to include a value from each cell in the *list* you specified for your selected operation. With one exception, which is noted below, the @AVG function ignores cells that are truly empty of data contents or formatting information. However, if your *list* contains any of the cell types noted below, each of these cells will contribute a zero value to the average and increase the statistical divisor by one unit. This decreases the computed average value.

-   Cells containing labels.

-   Cells containing a label prefix only, which seem empty but really are not.

-   Cells containing spaces.

- Blank cells that are explicitly included by name.

Examples

Suppose cell A4 is blank, and cells A1..A3 contain the values 10, 20, and 30. For this calculation, @AVG(A1..A3) would return a value of 20, which is the sum of the three cells included (10+20+30=60) divided by the number of cells (3). Similarly, @AVG(A1..A4) would return a value of 20, because the blank cell A4 would not be included in the calculations. However, @AVG(A1..A3,A4) would produce a value of 15, because here you have explicitly included cell A4 by name. This adds the value of zero to cell A4 (a label), and increases the @AVG divisor by one. The calculation becomes (10 + 20 + 30 + 0)/4, or 15.

See Also   These other statistical functions: @COUNT, @MAX, @MIN, @STD, @SUM, and @VAR.

@CELL

- **PURPOSE**   To determine the characteristics of a cell, a particularly useful function during automated macro operations.

- **SYNTAX**

   @CELL(*attribute,range*)

where

- *attribute* is one of the following ten strings, expressed in quotation marks:

   Address, Col, Contents, Filename, Format, Prefix, Protect, Row, Type, or Width,

- and *range* is any cell name or range specifier.

- **NOTES**   If the *range* you've specified exceeds a single cell, the @CELL function returns information about the cell in the upper-left corner of the range. Since worksheet changes do not necessarily force recalculations, your @CELL references can become out of date. You can always press F9 to recalculate your worksheet, but macro usage requires a little more care. The @CELL function is used mostly in macros, so you must remember to first run the {CALC}, {RECALC}, or {RECALCCOL} macros to ensure that @CELL returns the most current information about the cell you specified.

Examples

Suppose your payroll deductions macro required users to enter data in a cell named WAGES. To make sure they do so, you could first place a user prompt in cell D8, by storing the following @IF function in cell D8:

@IF(@CELL("type",WAGES)="b","Please Enter Wages","OK")

This instance of the @CELL function would return a "type" code of "b"—in other words, blank—if no dollar amount had yet been entered into the WAGES cell. If you then write a macro such as

{IF (D8) = "OK"}{QUIT}
{GOTO}WAGES~

the macro code sequence moves the cell pointer to the WAGES cell.

See Also   These other functions: @?, @@, @CELLPOINTER, @CHOOSE, @COLS, @ERR, @HLOOKUP, @INDEX, @NA, @ROWS, and @VLOOKUP.

@CELLPOINTER

● **PURPOSE**   To obtain information about the current location of the cell pointer.

● **SYNTAX**

@CELLPOINTER(*attribute*)

where *attribute* is one of the following ten strings, expressed in quotation marks: Address, Col, Contents, Filename, Format, Prefix, Protect, Row, Type, and Width.

● **NOTES**   @CELLPOINTER returns the attribute of the cell that contains the cell pointer, not the attribute of the cell containing the @CELLPOINTER function itself. Use this function to control macro processing based on the actual location or contents of the cell.

However, @CELLPOINTER references may become out of date, because worksheet changes do not necessarily force recalculations. You can always press F9 to recalculate your worksheet, but macro usage requires a little more care. The @CELLPOINTER function is used mostly in macros, so you must remember to run the {CALC}, {RECALC}, or {RECALCCOL} macros first to ensure that @CELLPOINTER returns the most up-to-date information about the specified cell.

Examples

In macros that process a variable number of user inputs, with each input entered into a new row, you could use the @CELLPOINTER function to find out what row the user is up to. If the user has entered data into cell D19, for example, @CELLPOINTER("row") would return a value of 19.

See Also   These other special functions: @?, @@, @CELL, @CHOOSE, @COLS, @ERR, @HLOOKUP, @INDEX, @NA, @ROWS, and @VLOOKUP.

@CHAR

● **PURPOSE**   To convert a number to its equivalent LICS (Lotus International Character Set) entry character.

• SYNTAX

@CHAR(*n*)

where *n* is an integer or any 1-2-3 value that results in an integer. Integers can range from 1 to 255.

• **NOTES**   If *n* does not correspond to a LICS entry, 1-2-3 returns a value of ERR. Not all printers can print non-standard characters, nor can all screens display them, so the international and scientific characters in the Lotus International Character Set may look different on your screen or on your printouts.

Examples

Suppose you wanted to include the currency symbol of the Netherlands, the guilder, in a printout. To do this, you would use @CHAR(160) to display an italic *f*, which stands for the *floren*, the original currency name of the guilder.

Since the @CHAR function returns a string, you could create a string formula to combine special characters with conventional string sequences. For example, to produce a copyright message like this one:

Copyright (©) 1991 Computer Options

you would enter the following string formula:

+"Copyright "&@CHAR(169)&" 1991 Computer Options"

See Also   These other string functions: @CLEAN, @CODE, @EXACT, @FIND, @LEFT, @LENGTH, @LOWER, @MID, @N, @PROPER, @REPEAT, @REPLACE, @RIGHT, @S, @STRING, @TRIM, @UPPER, and @VALUE.

@CHOOSE

• **PURPOSE**   To obtain the *n*th entry in a list of 1-2-3 cells.

• SYNTAX

@CHOOSE(*n,list*)

where

- *n* is an offset number, beginning with 0, that 1-2-3 will use to select an entry from *list*; and

- *list* is any group of one or more 1-2-3 cell names, actual values, or labels.

• NOTES
@CHOOSE uses an *n* value of 0 to select the first item in the list, an *n* value of 1 to select the second, and so on. You cannot use a range name in the *list*: it must contain the actual list of items from which to make a choice.

Examples

Suppose you defined a table of month names—"January", "February", "March", and so on—in cells E3..E14. Furthermore, suppose that cell B8 contained a formula that computes a month (1 to 12). In order to obtain the actual character version of the month, you could choose one of the twelve entries with this formula:

@CHOOSE(B8–1,E3,E4,E5,E6,E7,E8,E9,E10,E11,E12,E13,E14)

If cell B8 contained 4, representing the fourth calendar month, then @CHOOSE would use B8–1 (4–1, or 3) to select the E6 entry in the list. The entire @CHOOSE function reference would return the string "April", found in cell E6.

See Also
The table lookup functions @HLOOKUP, @INDEX, and @VLOOKUP, and these other special functions: @?, @@, @CELL, @CELLPOINTER, @COLS, @ERR, @NA, and @ROWS.

@CLEAN

• PURPOSE
To remove certain specialized character codes from a string prior to printing or exporting the cell information.

• SYNTAX

@CLEAN(*string*)

where *string* is any 1-2-3 text data, a string function or formula, a cell address containing text, or a string enclosed in double quotation marks.

• NOTES

The @CLEAN function returns the original *string* and removes the following special codes:

- All control codes below ASCII 32.

- LICS merge code 155 and the following character.

- Begin and end attribute characters (LICS codes 151 and 152) and the intervening attribute character itself.

Examples

Suppose that you imported a delimited text file from a word processing or database program and unusual formatting or control characters were embedded in some of the fields. If cell F4, for example, appeared odd or was partially obscured by control characters, you could remove them with the @CLEAN function. @CLEAN(F4) would return the string from F4 without any of the problem characters—typically control codes with ASCII values below 32. Most likely, you would import several columns at a time. For each column, you could create a new column of @CLEAN formulas to re-create the text data without the obstructing codes.

See Also These other string functions: @CHAR, @CODE, @EXACT, @FIND, @LEFT, @LENGTH, @LOWER, @MID, @N, @PROPER, @REPEAT, @REPLACE, @RIGHT, @S, @STRING, @TRIM, @UPPER, and @VALUE.

@CODE

• PURPOSE

To obtain the LICS (Lotus International Character Set) code corresponding to the first character of any string.

• SYNTAX

@CODE(*string*)

where *string* is any 1-2-3 text string.

Examples

Suppose you imported a series of text strings from a word process-ing program, and the first character of each string defined a control code used by the original word processor to specify formatting in-formation. You wouldn't want to use @CLEAN to remove these codes until you could identify them and their original purpose. However, if the strings were in column C, for example, you could construct a series of formulas in column D to return the LICS codes for each format character in the corresponding column C cell: @CODE(C1), @CODE(C2), and so on.

See Also These other string functions: @CHAR, @CLEAN, @EXACT, @FIND, @LEFT, @LENGTH, @LOWER, @MID, @N, @PROPER, @REPEAT, @REPLACE, @RIGHT, @S, @STRING, @TRIM, @UPPER, and @VALUE.

@COLS

• PURPOSE   To determine the number of columns in a range of cells.

• SYNTAX

@COLS(*range*)

where *range* is any 1-2-3 range name or address.

• NOTES   Use this function in macros to determine how many currently existing columns in a changing range should be processed.

Examples

Suppose that your ongoing budget analysis used the actual expenditures stored in a range called ACTUALS. This range could span a number of columns, ranging from 1 to 12 months. If you entered data for January, February, March, and April, and ACTUALS now spanned B4..E10—in other words, seven budgeting categories in rows 4 to 10, and four months in columns B to E—the @COLS(ACTUALS) function would return a value of 4. This value could then be used by the automated macro to repeat some printing or analysis logic this variable (four) number of times.

See Also   These other special functions: @?, @@, @CELL, @CELLPOINTER, @CHOOSE, @ERR, @HLOOKUP, @INDEX, @NA, @ROWS, and @VLOOKUP.

@COS

● **PURPOSE**   To calculate the cosine of an angle.

● **SYNTAX**

@COS(*x*)

where *x* is a 1-2-3 value representing the angle in radians.

● **NOTES** X can have any value. Remember that there are 2 π radians in 360 degrees. You can convert from degrees to the necessary angle in radians by using the @PI function

Angle in Radians = @PI/180 * Angle in Degrees

The @COS function returns a cosine value from −1 to +1.

Examples

Suppose *x* equals 60 degrees. You can first convert that to radians by multiplying 60 times @PI and dividing by 180. This returns 1.047197. The @COS(1.047197) function returns the expected value of 0.5.

If cell C1 contains an angle in degrees of 30, the following formula in cell C2 would result in 0.523598:

@PI/180*C1

A final formula in cell C3 of @COS(C2) would produce the cosine of 30 degrees, or 0.866025.

See Also   These other mathematical functions: @ABS, @ACOS, @ASIN, @ATAN, @ATAN2, @EXP, @INT, @LN, @LOG, @MOD, @PI, @RAND, @ROUND, @SIN, @SQRT, and @TAN.

@COUNT

● **PURPOSE**   To count the number of non-blank cells in a group of 1-2-3 cells.

● **SYNTAX**

@COUNT(*list*)

where *list* is any series of 1-2-3 cells or range names separated by commas.

● **NOTES**   Be careful when you include cell names and ranges in your *list*. Statistical functions attempt to include each cell in the *list* you specify for your selected operation. With one exception, which is noted below, the @COUNT function ignores cells that are truly empty of data contents or formatting information. However, if your *list* contains any of the following type cells, each of those cells will contribute a count of 1 to the total count:

- Cells containing labels.

- Cells containing a label prefix only, which seem empty but really are not.

- Cells containing spaces.

- Cells containing undefined range names.

- Cells containing ERR or NA values.

- Blank cells that are explicitly included by name.

Examples

Suppose cell A4 is blank, and cells A1..A3 contain the values 10, 20, and 30. For this calculation, @COUNT(A1..A3) would return a value of 3, which is the actual number of cells included. @COUNT(A1..A4) would similarly return a value of 3 because the included blank cell A4 would not be included in the actual calculations. However, @COUNT(A1..A3,A4) would produce a value of 4, because here you explicitly included cell A4 by name. This adds a count of 1 to the total count.

See Also   These other statistical functions: @AVG, @MAX, @MIN, @STD, @SUM, and @VAR.

@CTERM

- **PURPOSE**   To calculate the compounding term—the number of compounding periods—required for an investment quantity to grow to a specified larger amount, given a fixed rate of interest per compounding period.

- **SYNTAX**

    @CTERM(*interest,FutureValue,PresentValue*)

where

- *interest* is a 1-2-3 value, expressed in decimal or percentage form, that represents the periodic interest rate; and

- *FutureValue* is a 1-2-3 value that represents the desired eventual value of the investment specified by *PresentValue*.

- **NOTES**   Both *FutureValue* and *PresentValue* must be positive or negative at the same time, thereby representing a growing or declining investment.

Remember to enter the *interest* rate for each compounding period, rather than simply for the commonly expressed annual percentage rate. The value for *interest* must be numerically greater than −1.

Examples

Suppose, at age 45, you deposit $10,000 into an interest bearing retirement account. You're hoping to triple your money by the time you retire. @CTERM can tell you how long it will be before the investment triples in worth. At a 7% annual rate, the monthly—that is the compounding period—interest is .07/12, so the formula to use is

@CTERM(.07/12,30000,10000)

This results in the number of compounding periods (188.88). Dividing by twelve produces a more meaningful answer of 15.74, the number of years to triple the investment.

See Also These other financial functions: @DDB, @FV, @IRR, @NPV, @PMT, @PV, @RATE, @SLN, @SYD, and @TERM.

@DATE

- **PURPOSE** To calculate the 1-2-3 date value corresponding to a date specified by year, month, and day values.

- **SYNTAX**

  ### @DATE(*year,month,day*)

where

- *year* is a 1-2-3 value, ranging from 0 to 199, which represents the offset from the year 1900 (for example, 27 represents 1927);

- *month* is a 1-2-3 value, ranging from 1 to 12, which represents the month of the year; and

- *day* is a 1-2-3 value, ranging from 1 to 31, which represents a valid day of the month.

● **NOTES**   *Day* must be within the correct number of days for the specified *month* and *year*.

The value returned by @DATE is a decimal number. You must use /Range Format if you wish this value to actually appear as a date on your worksheet.

Examples

Suppose that your worksheet has three named ranges: YEAR, MONTH, and DAY. If YEAR contains 91, MONTH contains 6, and DAY contains 15, then @DATE(YEAR,MONTH,DAY) returns 33404. If you format this cell with /Range Format Date 1, then the date value appears as 15-Jun-91.

See Also   These other date and time functions: @DATEVALUE, @DAY, @HOUR, @MINUTE, @MONTH, @NOW, @SECOND, @TIME, @TIMEVALUE, and @YEAR.

@DATEVALUE

● **PURPOSE**   To calculate the 1-2-3 date value corresponding to a date expressed as a text string.

● **SYNTAX**

@DATEVALUE(*string*)

where *string* is any 1-2-3 label, text formula, or cell identifier containing either of these.

● **NOTES**   *String* must be expressed in one of the five allowable formats shown in the /Range Format Date command. Use this function when you import text data from other programs, or when you wish to convert text strings found in other cells for the purpose of calculating date functions.

The value returned by @DATEVALUE is a decimal number. You must use /Range Format if you wish this value to actually appear as a date on your worksheet.

Examples

If your anniversary fell on June 15, 1991, and cell B1 contained "6/15/91", then @DATEVALUE(B1) would return 33404.

See Also   These other date and time functions: @DATE, @DAY, @HOUR, @MINUTE, @MONTH, @NOW, @SECOND, @TIME, @TIMEVALUE, and @YEAR.

@DAVG

- **PURPOSE**   To obtain the average value of some or all of the entries in one column of a database table.

- **SYNTAX**

  @DAVG(*database,field,criteria*)

where

- *database* identifies a cell range, by name or address, that represents a 1-2-3 database table.

- *field* is a 1-2-3 value that represents the offset number of the table column to use. Offset 0 is the first column, or field, in the database table.

- *criteria* identifies a 1-2-3 cell range that contains two or more rows. The first row contains field names from the database table for which selection conditions will be specified. The remaining rows in the criteria range contain the actual conditions for each specified database field name.

• NOTES Leave the second row of the criteria range blank if you wish to average all the records (rows) in a database. Extend the criteria range to include additional rows if you wish to apply more criteria to the averaging logic.

Examples

Suppose your worksheet contained a database of employee information located in a named range called EMPLOYEE. The third column (offset 2) was the label "PAYRATE". As part of a management wage review, you were asked to compare the average salaries paid to married and single employees. Naturally, if you also needed to obtain the average salary of all employees, you could include them all in the calculations simply by leaving the second row of the criteria range blank; this would impose no criteria constraints on the EMPLOYEE table.

Your criteria range spanned A12..D13 because your EMPLOYEE table included columns for ID, NAME, PAYRATE, and marital STATUS. You could average the salary figures for just the married employees in the following way. Assuming that the married employees were identified by an entry called "Married" in the STATUS column, you could type a criterion label of "Married" in row two of the criteria range. This would be cell D13, if the criteria range began with column headings in row 12. If three married employees in your small firm earned $2200, $2100, and $2435, then the formula

@DAVG(EMPLOYEE,2,A12..D13)

would return a $2245 average salary for married employees. The same formula would instantly return the average salary of single employees as well—after you had replaced "Married" in cell D13 with "Single".

See Also These other database functions: @DCOUNT, @DMAX, @DMIN, @DSTD, @DSUM, and @DVAR.

@DAY

● **PURPOSE** To obtain the day of the month for the date represented by a 1-2-3 date value.

● **SYNTAX**

@DAY(*datenumber*)

where *datenumber* is a 1-2-3 value that ranges from an offset number of days from January 1, 1900 through December 31, 2099. The number 1 represents 1/1/1900 and the maximum value 73050 represents 12/31/2099.

● **NOTES** Use this function to obtain, for subsequent date calculations, the numeric day in a particular month.

Examples

If cell B2 contained 33404, which is the 1-2-3 date value for June 15, 1991, then @DAY(B2) would result in the value 15.

See Also These other date and time functions: @DATE, @DATEVALUE, @HOUR, @MINUTE, @MONTH, @NOW, @SECOND, @TIME, @TIMEVALUE, and @YEAR.

@DCOUNT

● **PURPOSE** To count how many row entries exist in a database, subject to specified criteria.

● **SYNTAX**

@DCOUNT(*database,field,criteria*)

where

- *database* identifies a cell range, by name or address, that represents a 1-2-3 database table.

- *field* is a 1-2-3 value that represents the offset number of the table column to use. Offset 0 is the first column, or field, in the database table.

- *criteria* identifies a 1-2-3 cell range that contains two or more rows. The first row contains field names from the database table for which selection conditions will be specified. The remaining rows in the criteria range contain the actual conditions for each specified database field name.

- **NOTES**   Leave the second row of the criteria range blank if you wish to count all the records (rows) in a database. Extend the criteria range to include additional rows if you wish to apply more criteria to the counting logic.

Examples

Suppose that your worksheet contained a database of employee information located in a named range called EMPLOYEE, with the first column (offset 0) simply the employee ID. You could include all employees in the result if you left the second row of the criteria range blank; this would impose no criteria constraints on the EMPLOYEE table. If the criteria range spanned A12..D13, perhaps because your EMPLOYEE table included columns for ID, NAME, PAYRATE, and marital STATUS, the following formula would return 6 if your EMPLOYEE table contained six entries, and 600 if the table contained six hundred entries:

@DCOUNT(EMPLOYEE,0,A12..D13)

Suppose that you wanted to find out how many employees earned more than $2000 per pay period. You would enter the text condition ">2000" in the second row of the criteria range just below the column heading PAYRATE. The same formula would then return 4, if only four employees were at this larger salary level.

See Also   These other database functions: @DAVG, @DMAX, @DMIN, @DSTD, @DSUM, and @DVAR.

@DDB

● **PURPOSE** To compute the accelerated depreciation allowance of an asset, using the double-declining balance method.

● **SYNTAX**

@DDB(*startvalue,endvalue,life,period*)

where

- *startvalue* is a 1-2-3 value that represents the initial cost of the asset.

- *endvalue* is a 1-2-3 value that represents the estimated salvage value of the asset at the end of its useful life.

- *life* is the number of periods the asset takes to depreciate from *initialvalue* to *endvalue*.

- *period* is the specific time period for which you wish to calculate the double-declining balance depreciation allowance.

● **NOTES** Use this function when you wish to reduce tax liability by a greater amount in the early years of your asset's life, when the depreciation allowance is greater. @DDB uses the following formula to calculate depreciation:

2*BookValue/life

where *BookValue* = *Startvalue* $-\Sigma$ (the prior period's depreciation).

Examples

Suppose you bought an office copier for $25,000. You assume from experience that you will replace it in five years, and that you will be able to resell it at that time for $10,000. You wish to write off the largest possible amount of this asset in the first year because you've earned extra income. You choose @DDB (versus straight line or sum-of-the-years'-digits), because you quickly discover that the first year's depreciation allowance is @DDB(25000,10000,5,1), or $10,000. Repeating this formula for years 2 through 5—changing only the last argument value—shows the reducing depreciation amounts of $5000, $0, $0, $0, all of which add up to a total depreciation allowance of $15,000. Importantly, however, two thirds of the depreciable amount is obtained in the first year alone using this method.

See Also These other financial functions: @CTERM, @FV, @IRR, @NPV, @PMT, @PV, @RATE, @SLN, @SYD, and @TERM.

@DMAX

● **PURPOSE** To obtain the largest columnar value in a database table, or in a selected set of rows from that table.

● **SYNTAX**

@DMAX(*database,field,criteria*)

where

- *database* identifies a cell range, by name or address, that represents a 1-2-3 database table.

- *field* is a 1-2-3 value that represents the offset number of the table column to use. Offset 0 is the first column, or field, in the database table.

- *criteria* identifies a 1-2-3 cell range that contains two or more rows. The first row contains field names from the database table for which selection conditions will be specified. The remaining rows in the criteria range contain the actual conditions for each specified database field name.

● **NOTES** Leave the second row of the criteria range blank if you wish to include all columnar values in the evaluation. Extend the criteria range to include additional rows if you wish to apply more criteria, and thereby select only some rows for analysis.

Examples

Suppose that your worksheet contained a database of employee information located in a named range called EMPLOYEE. The third
column (offset 2) was the employee PAYRATE. You could include all
employees in the analysis by leaving the second row of the criteria
range blank; this would impose no criteria constraints on the
EMPLOYEE table. Assuming that the criteria range spanned A12..D13,
and that the EMPLOYEE table included columns for ID, NAME,
PAYRATE, and marital STATUS, you could obtain the largest salary
figure for any employee by leaving row two of the criteria range completely blank. In this way, the following formula would return the
largest value in the third column (PAYRATE) of the database table:

@DMAX(EMPLOYEE,2,A12..D13)

See Also   These other database functions: @DAVG, @DCOUNT,
@DMIN, @DSTD, @DSUM, and @DVAR.

@DMIN

• PURPOSE   To obtain the smallest columnar value in a database table, or in a selected set of rows from that table.

• SYNTAX

@DMIN(*database,field,criteria*)

where

- *database* identifies a cell range, by name or address, that
  represents a 1-2-3 database table.

- *field* is a 1-2-3 value that represents the offset number of
  the table column to use. Offset 0 is the first column, or
  field, in the database table.

- *criteria* identifies a 1-2-3 cell range that contains two or
  more rows. The first row contains field names from the

database table for which selection conditions will be specified. The remaining rows in the criteria range contain the actual conditions for each specified database field name.

● **NOTES**   Leave the second row of the criteria range blank if you wish to include all columnar values in the evaluation. Extend the criteria range to include additional rows if you wish to apply more criteria, and thereby select only some rows for analysis.

Examples

Suppose that your worksheet contained a database of employee information located in a named range called EMPLOYEE, and the third column (offset 2) was the employee PAYRATE. You could include all employees in the analysis by leaving the second row of the criteria range blank; this would impose no criteria constraints on the EMPLOYEE table.

Assuming that the criteria range spanned A12..D13, and that the EMPLOYEE table included columns for ID, NAME, PAYRATE, and marital STATUS, you could obtain the smallest salary figure of all the employees by leaving row two of the criteria range completely blank. In this way, the following formula would return the smallest value in the third column (PAYRATE) of the database table:

@DMIN(EMPLOYEE,2,A12..D13)

See Also   These other database functions: @DAVG, @DCOUNT, @DMAX, @DSTD, @DSUM, and @DVAR.

@DSTD

● **PURPOSE**   To obtain the standard deviation of some or all of the entries in one column of a database table.

● **SYNTAX**

@DSTD(*database,field,criteria*)

where

- *database* identifies a cell range, by name or address, that represents a 1-2-3 database table.

- *field* is a 1-2-3 value that represents the offset number of the table column to use. Offset 0 is the first column, or field, in the database table.

- *criteria* identifies a 1-2-3 cell range that contains two or more rows. The first row contains field names from the database table for which selection conditions will be specified. The remaining rows in the criteria range contain the actual conditions for each specified database field name.

● **NOTES**   When computing the standard deviation of any list of values, 1-2-3 uses the same *n* (population) method for computing standard deviation in a database table as it does in the @STD function. See the @STD entry for a more detailed explanation of standard deviation.

Leave the second row of the criteria range blank if you wish to analyze all the records (rows) in a database. Extend the criteria range to include additional rows if you wish to include only some of the rows in the standard deviation list.

Examples

Suppose that your worksheet contained a database of employee information located in a named range called EMPLOYEE, and the third column (offset 2) was the label "PAYRATE". As part of a management wage review, you were asked to compute the standard deviation of both the married and single employee pay rates separately. Naturally, if you also needed to obtain an overall figure for all employees, you could include them all in the calculations by leaving the second row of the criteria range blank; this would impose no criteria constraints on the EMPLOYEE table.

If the criteria range spanned A12..D13, perhaps because your EMPLOYEE table included columns for ID, NAME, PAYRATE, and marital STATUS, you could compute standard deviation for just the married employees in the following way. Assuming that the married employees are identified by an entry called "Married" in the

STATUS column, you could type a criterion label of "Married" in row two of the criteria range. This would be cell D13, if the criteria range began with column headings in row 12. If three married employees in your small firm earned $2200, $2100, and $2435, then the formula

@DSTD(EMPLOYEE,2,A12..D13)

would return a standard deviation value of 140.416 for married employee pay rates. The same formula would instantly return the standard deviation for single employees as well—after you replaced "Married" in cell D13 with "Single".

See Also @STD, and these other database functions: @DAVG, @DCOUNT, @DMAX, @DMIN, @DSUM, and @DVAR.

@DSUM

● **PURPOSE** To add up all or some of the values in one column of a database table.

● **SYNTAX**

@DSUM(*database,field,criteria*)

where

- *database* identifies a cell range, by name or address, that represents a 1-2-3 database table.

- *field* is a 1-2-3 value that represents the offset number of the table column to use. Offset 0 is the first column, or field, in the database table.

- *criteria* identifies a 1-2-3 cell range that contains two or more rows. The first row contains field names from the database table for which selection conditions will be specified. The remaining rows in the criteria range contain the actual conditions for each specified database field name.

● **NOTES**   Leave the second row of the criteria range blank if you wish to add up the columnar entries from all the records (rows) in a database. Extend the criteria range to include additional rows if you wish to include only some of the rows in the summation.

Examples

Suppose that your worksheet contained a database of employee information located in a named range called EMPLOYEE, and the third column (offset 2) was the label "PAYRATE". As part of a cash flow analysis, you were asked to determine the current payroll commitment. You could include all employees in the required summation simply by leaving the second row of the criteria range blank; this would impose no criteria constraints on the EMPLOYEE table. If the criteria range spanned A12..D13—perhaps because your EMPLOYEE table included columns for ID, NAME, PAYRATE, and marital STATUS—you could compute the total dollars required to meet payroll with the following formula:

@DSUM(EMPLOYEE,2,A12..D13)

See Also   These other database functions: @DAVG, @DCOUNT, @DMAX, @DMIN, @DSTD, and @DVAR.

@DVAR

● **PURPOSE**   To obtain the population variance of some or all of the entries in one column of a database table.

● **SYNTAX**

@DVAR(*database,field,criteria*)

where

- *database* identifies a cell range, by name or address, that represents a 1-2-3 database table.

- *field* is a 1-2-3 value that represents the offset number of the table column to use. Offset 0 is the first column, or field, in the database table.

- *criteria* identifies a 1-2-3 cell range that contains two or more rows. The first row contains field names from the database table for which selection conditions will be specified. The remaining rows in the criteria range contain the actual conditions for each specified database field name.

● NOTES   When computing the variance of any list of values, 1-2-3 uses the same n (population) method for computing variance in a database table as it does in the @VAR function. See the @VAR entry for a more detailed explanation of variance.

Leave the second row of the criteria range blank if you wish to analyze all the records (rows) in a database. Extend the criteria range to include additional rows if you wish to include only some of the rows in the variance list.

Examples

Suppose that your worksheet contained a database of employee information located in a named range called EMPLOYEE, and the third column (offset 2) was the label PAYRATE. As part of a management wage review, you were asked to compute the variance of both the married and single employee pay rates separately. Naturally, if you also needed to obtain an overall figure for all employees, you could include them all in the calculations simply by leaving the second row of the criteria range blank; this would impose no criteria constraints on the EMPLOYEE table.

If the criteria range spanned A12..D13—perhaps because your EMPLOYEE table included columns for ID, NAME, PAYRATE, and marital STATUS—you could compute variance for just the married employees in the following way. Assuming that the married employees were identified by an entry called "Married" in the STATUS column, you could type a criterion label called "Married" in row two of the criteria range. This would be cell D13, if the criteria range began with column headings in row 12. If three married employees in your small firm earned $2200, $2100, and $2435, then the formula

@DVAR(EMPLOYEE,2,A12..D13)

would return a variance value of 19716.66 for married employee pay rates. The same formula would instantly return the variance for single employees as well—after you replaced "Married" in cell D13 with "Single".

See Also @VAR, and these other database functions: @DAVG, @DCOUNT, @DMAX, @DMIN, @DSTD, and @DSUM.

@ERR

- **PURPOSE** To produce the special cell value ERR.

- **SYNTAX**

  @ERR

- **NOTES** Use @ERR to indicate some error to the worksheet user. If one cell evaluates to ERR, all formulas that depend on that cell also evaluate to ERR.

Note that ERR is a unique character display that represents a special 1-2-3 value; it is not equivalent to the label "ERR", which would otherwise look the same in the cell.

Examples

Suppose that a user is expected to enter an employee's weekly wages into a cell named WAGES. The following formula would display an unobtrusive blank space if the salary amount is within guidelines—that is, if it is under $1500—but would display ERR if the amount exceeded this logical limit:

@IF(WAGES>1500,@ERR," ")

See Also These other special functions: @?, @@, @CELL, @CELLPOINTER, @CHOOSE, @COLS, @HLOOKUP, @INDEX, @NA, @ROWS, and @VLOOKUP.

@EXACT

- **PURPOSE** To provide a more precise comparison between two 1-2-3 string expressions than is offered by the simple equality sign (=).

- **SYNTAX**

  @EXACT(*string1*,*string2*)

where *string1* is any 1-2-3 text string, and *string2* is any 1-2-3 text string.

- **NOTES** If *string1* is an exact replica (in both contents and length) of *string2*, @EXACT returns a numeric value of 1, which means TRUE. Otherwise, @EXACT returns a value of 0, or FALSE.

The equal operator does not distinguish between upper- and lower-case letters; the @EXACT function does distinguish between upper- and lowercase characters. In addition, @EXACT detects the difference between accented and unaccented foreign letters.

Examples

Suppose that your worksheet contained a named range called START, which is included for password entry by users during a particular macro's execution. If your password was the four character upper- and lowercase sequence "JuDd", then the following macro sequence would only QUIT if the user entered the correct upper- and lowercase character sequence:

```
{IF @exact(start,"JuDd")=1}{QUIT}
{GOTO}start
```

If a user did not correctly enter the password during macro execution, the {GOTO} instruction in the second line would force the cell pointer to the START cell. There you could display another prompt to request user entry.

On the other hand, if you had used a simple equality operation, such as

    {IF start="JuDd"}{QUIT}
    {GOTO}start

then a user entry of "JUDD" would slip through the test.

See Also   These other string functions: @CHAR, @CLEAN, @CODE, @FIND, @LEFT, @LENGTH, @LOWER, @MID, @N, @PROPER, @REPEAT, @REPLACE, @RIGHT, @S, @STRING, @TRIM, @UPPER, and @VALUE.

@EXP

* **PURPOSE**   To raise *e* (approximately 2.718282) to a power.

* **SYNTAX**

    @EXP(*x*)

where *x* is a 1-2-3 value representing a numeric power to which the mathematical constant *e* is to be raised.

* **NOTES**   *X* can't be larger than 709, since the calculation would then exceed 1-2-3's ability to store the result. Furthermore, if *x* exceeds 230, or is smaller than –227, 1-2-3 can compute the result but can't display it. In this case, 1-2-3 would display a series of asterisks in the cell. The limit for scientific display notation in 1-2-3 is 9.9E99.

Examples

If *x* equals 3, then @EXP(3) would return a value of 20.08553. If cell C1 contained a formula that evaluated to a value of 200, then @EXP(C1) would result in 7.2E+86.

See Also   These other mathematical functions: @ABS, @ACOS, @ASIN, @ATAN, @ATAN2, @COS, @INT, @LN, @LOG, @MOD, @PI, @RAND, @ROUND, @SIN, @SQRT, and @TAN.

@FALSE

● **PURPOSE**   To return a logical value of FALSE, which is equivalent to 1-2-3's numeric value of 0.

● **SYNTAX**

@FALSE

Examples

Suppose that some other worksheet cell (a range named OKENTRY) tested whether or not cell A1 contained a value greater than 350:

@IF(A1<350,@TRUE,@FALSE)

This would result in range OKENTRY containing the number 1 (logical value TRUE) if A1 contained 350 or less. Range OKENTRY would contain the number 0 (logical value FALSE) if A1 equalled 350 or more. Elsewhere on your worksheet, you could have a formula that tests the range OKENTRY:

@IF(OKENTRY=@FALSE,"REENTER DATA"," ")

Because you used a test involving @FALSE, rather than an equivalent test for 0, the processing logic would be easier to read and understand. If the data entry were not right, the prompt "REENTER DATA" would appear; other macro controlled processing could then return the cell pointer to cell A1 for the actual data reentry.

See Also   These other Logical functions: @IF, @ISAAF, @ISAPP, @ISERR, @ISNA, @ISNUMBER, @ISSTRING, and @TRUE.

@FIND

- **PURPOSE**   To determine the location of a *substring*, or one string of characters, within another string.

- **SYNTAX**

   @FIND(*substring,string,start*)

where

- *substring* is any 1-2-3 string expression;

- *string* is any 1-2-3 string expression; and

- *start* is any 1-2-3 value that represents the starting offset position within *string* at which the search for a match of the *substring* character sequence is to begin.

- **NOTES**   The sequence of characters in *substring* cannot be longer than that in *string*. *Start* cannot be negative, or an offset that would begin beyond the length of *string*. 1-2-3 returns a value of ERR if these situations exist, or if the specified *substring* cannot be found within *string*.

@FIND is often used in text extraction or replacement to locate the starting position of a substring just prior to using the @MID or @REPLACE functions.

If *substring* appears more than once in the specified *string*, only the first appearance is identified by the return value of the function.

Examples

Let's suppose that cell A2 contained the string "415-524-0524". @FIND("524",A2,0) would result in the number 4 because the first occurrence of substring "524" was found within the longer string

"415-524-0524" beginning at offset position 4. Remember that, in 1-2-3 functions like this one, offsets always begin with 0, then 1, then 2, and so on. So the fifth position in the *string* is really identified as offset location number 4.

See Also These other string functions: @CHAR, @CLEAN, @CODE, @EXACT, @LEFT, @LENGTH, @LOWER, @MID, @N, @PROPER, @REPEAT, @REPLACE, @RIGHT, @S, @STRING, @TRIM, @UPPER, and @VALUE.

@FV

● **PURPOSE** To compute the future value of an investment that consists of a series of regular payments, over a fixed number of compounding periods, and at a specific interest rate.

● **SYNTAX**

@FV(*payment,interest,term*)

where

- *payment* is a 1-2-3 value representing the dollar amount invested each period;

- *interest* is a 1-2-3 value, expressed in decimal or percentage form, that represents the periodic interest rate; and

- *term* is a 1-2-3 value that represents the number of payment periods.

● **NOTES** The @FV function uses the following formula to return a value:

$$payment * \{[(1 + interest)^{term} - 1] / interest\}$$

This formula assumes that the payment is made at the very end of each compounding period. If the payment is made at the beginning of the period, as is done with annuity payments, the future value will be greater. To obtain this larger value, you should multiply the return value from the function by the quantity *(1 + interest)*.

Examples

Suppose that your son will be going to college in four years. If you plan to save $250 each month, the @FV function can tell you how much money your investment will be worth when he enters college. Assuming that there are forty-eight months left to save, and that your savings method pays a 7.5% annual interest, you will have $13,943.97 in the account in four years, as given by this formula:

@FV(250,.075/12,48)

Remember to divide the annual interest rate, which is expressed as a decimal, by 12 to adjust it to the monthly rate, in correspondence with the compounding periods that are expressed in months (48).

See Also   These other financial functions: @CTERM, @DDB, @IRR, @NPV, @PMT, @PV, @RATE, @SLN, @SYD, and @TERM.

@HLOOKUP

● **PURPOSE**   To obtain the contents of a cell from a table, given a row selector and a column selector.

● **SYNTAX**

@HLOOKUP(*column,range,row*)

where

- *column* is a value or string used to determine which column of the table to select from.

- *range* is the total extent of the 1-2-3 cell range that constitutes the table. The first row of the table is called the *index row* and contains the row headings against which the *column* argument will be compared.

- *row* contains the row offset to be used to look up an entry in the table. Row 0 is the index row, making rows 1, 2, 3 and so on the actual data rows in the table.

● **NOTES**   Use @HLOOKUP when you wish to look up an entry in a table based on a specifically known value or label.

The *column* selector can be any 1-2-3 quantity that evaluates to a value or a string. @HLOOKUP compares the *column* selector data against the entries in the first row of the table *range*. If the *column* entry contains a text string, @HLOOKUP will expect to find that precise string in the top row of the table *range*. If the *column* entry is a value, @HLOOKUP chooses the column headed by that value, or by a value just below the value specified.

Remember that the *row* argument is an offset number used to determine which row is to be used from the table; it is not an actual 1-2-3 worksheet row number, such as 1 to 8196.

Examples

Take a look at Figure III.1. The cell *range* D4..G15 is named RATES, and represents a sample table of insurance rates for men in the age range 30 to 40. A prospective customer's age is entered in cell B5,

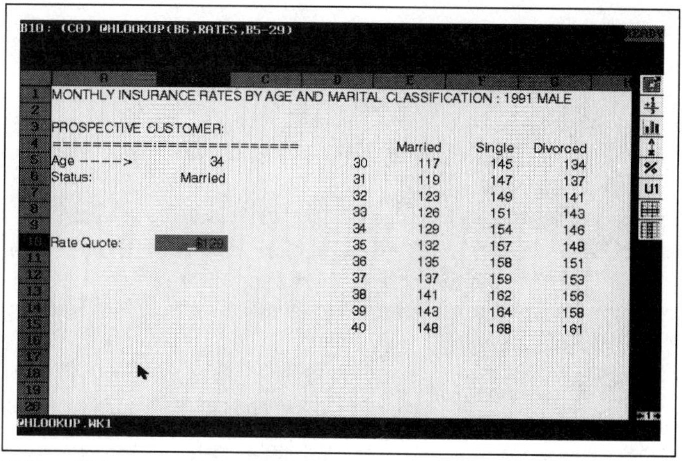

Figure III.1: The horizontal lookup function

and his marital status is entered in cell B6. The rate quote appears in cell B10, and is obtained from the RATES table with the following function reference:

@HLOOKUP(B6,RATES,B5–29)

The appropriate column is found by comparing the entry in cell B6, the Married column. The appropriate row offset is calculated by subtracting the base of the age range from the actual age (B5 – 29); for age 34, the offset points to row five of the table. The @HLOOKUP function returns the entry 129 found at the intersection of the specified *column* and *row* arguments.

See Also   The table lookup functions @CHOOSE, @INDEX, and VLOOKUP, and these other special functions: @?, @@, @CELL, @CELLPOINTER, @COLS, @ERR, @NA, and @ROWS.

@HOUR

- **PURPOSE**   To obtain the hour number (from 0 to 23) from a 1-2-3 decimal time number.

- **SYNTAX**

    @HOUR(*timevalue*)

where *timevalue* is a 1-2-3 value, ranging from .000000 through .999988, representing an offset number of seconds from midnight through 11:59:59P.M.

- **NOTES**   Use @HOUR in calculations involving the number of elapsed hours, such as those in payroll applications. *Timevalue* is typically obtained from formulas involving the @NOW, @TIME, or @TIMEVALUE functions.

Examples

Suppose an employee punches a time clock at 9:02A.M. and punches out at 5:04P.M.—@TIMEVALUE can obtain the precise time values. The @HOUR function can obtain the integer number for the hour of the day for the start and end times of these employee shifts. For example, @TIMEVALUE("9:02am") results in .376388, and @HOUR(.376388) results in 9. @TIMEVALUE("5:04pm") results in .711111, and @HOUR(.711111) results in 17, which represents the number of hours (seventeen) after midnight, or 5:00P.M.

See Also   These other date and time functions: @DATE, @DATE-VALUE, @DAY, @MINUTE, @MONTH, @NOW, @SECOND, @TIME, @TIMEVALUE, and @YEAR.

- **PURPOSE**   To evaluate a logical expression and return one of two values, depending on whether the expression is TRUE or FALSE.

- **SYNTAX**

  @IF(*condition,result1,result2***)**

where

- *condition* is any 1-2-3 logical formula, or a cell name or address, containing a logical formula;

- *result1* is any 1-2-3 value or label; and

- *result2* is any 1-2-3 value or label.

- **NOTES**   This is one of the most powerful, important, and often used functions in 1-2-3. It is used frequently in such activities as

- displaying one of two labels;

- displaying an error message or other indicator;

- returning different values for subsequent processing; and

- returning a value for processing, or a label for information.

Examples

Suppose that a user is expected to enter an employee's weekly wages into a cell named WAGES. The following formula would display an unobtrusive blank space if the salary amount is within guidelines—that is, if it is under $1500—but would display ERR if the amount exceeded this logical limit:

@IF(WAGES>1500,@ERR," ")

See Also   These other Logical functions: @FALSE, @ISAAF, @ISAPP, @ISERR, @ISNA, @ISNUMBER, @ISSTRING, and @TRUE.

@INDEX

- **PURPOSE**   To obtain a cell's contents, given its row and column offsets within a table of cells.

- **SYNTAX**

    @INDEX(*range,column,row*)

where

- *range* is the total extent of the 1-2-3 cell range that constitutes the table.

- *column* contains the column offset to be used to look up an entry in the table. Column 0 is the first column, usually containing the row labels, making columns 1, 2, 3 and so on the actual data columns in the table.

- *row* contains the row offset to be used to look up an entry in the table. Row 0 is the top row, usually containing the column headings, making rows 1, 2, 3 and so on the actual data rows in the table.

● **NOTES**   Use the @INDEX function when your table information can be extracted by position only, rather than by comparison with the row or column headings.

Examples

Look at Figure III.2. The cell *range* A2..D5, named SCHEDULE, represents a sample table of student course selections for required elective classes. Since both the choices and the electives are numbered, rather than named, the @INDEX function serves the selection purpose better than the @HLOOKUP (horizontal) or @VLOOKUP (vertical) table lookup functions. The requested table selection appears

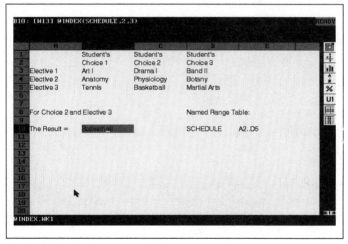

Figure III.2: An indexed table lookup

in cell B8, and is obtained from the SCHEDULE table with the following function reference:

@INDEX(SCHEDULE,2,3)

The appropriate column is found at offset 2 and the appropriate row is found at offset 3. The @INDEX function returns the entry "Basketball" found at the intersection of the specified *column* and *row* arguments.

See Also   The table lookup functions @CHOOSE, @HLOOKUP, and VLOOKUP, and these other special functions: @?, @@, @CELL, @CELLPOINTER, @COLS, @ERR, @NA, and @ROWS.

@INT

- **PURPOSE**   To obtain the integer portion only of a 1-2-3 value.

- **SYNTAX**

   @INT(x)

where *x* is any 1-2-3 value.

- **NOTES**   The @INT function obtains the integer portion of a value through truncation. Any decimal portion is dropped; the result is not rounded.

If you wish to retain the actual floating point—the decimal—value of a number, but wish to display only an integer, you should control cell formatting instead. The /Range Format Fixed 0 command adjusts the appearance of specific cells by showing only the integer portion. The /Worksheet Global Format Fixed 0 performs the same task for all worksheet cells that are not otherwise formatted with the /Range Format command.

Examples

If *x* equaled 2.389, then @INT(2.389) would return 2 as its resulting value. If cell C1 contained a formula that evaluated to a value of −287.56, then @INT(C1) would return −287 as its result.

See Also   /Range Format, /Worksheet Global, and these other mathematical functions: @ABS, @ACOS, @ASIN, @ATAN, @ATAN2, @COS, @EXP, @LN, @LOG, @MOD, @PI, @RAND, @ROUND, @SIN, @SQRT, and @TAN.

@IRR

● **PURPOSE**   To compute the internal rate of return for a series of cash investment inflows and outflows.

● **SYNTAX**

@IRR(*estimate,range*)

where

- *estimate* is your guess (between 0% and 100%) at the internal rate of return; and

- *range* is a 1-2-3 cell address or range name that contains cash flow values (negative numbers are outflows and positive numbers are inflows).

● **NOTES**   Usually, the first cell in the range contains a negative number representing the initial investment. Remaining numbers are positive and represent periodic payments to the investment.

Examples

Suppose you and forty other investors each invested $5000 in a startup company. The principals of the company promised to pay $300 a month for four years. Storing –5000 in cell A1, and 300 in cells A2..A49 to represent four years, or forty-eight months, of payments, you made a hopeful initial estimate of 10%. You calculated the internal rate of return of this investment to be @IRR(.10,A1..A49), or a disappointing value of 5.55%.

See Also These other financial functions: @CTERM, @DDB, @FV, @NPV, @PMT, @PV, @RATE, @SLN, @SYD, and @TERM.

@ISAAF

● **PURPOSE** To test whether or not a specified function name is valid for an attached 1-2-3 Add-In program.

● **SYNTAX**

@ISAAF(*name*)

where *name* is a 1-2-3 text string, formula, or reference to a cell containing a label. *Name* represents an add-in function name to be tested; do not use the @ prefix common to all functions.

● **NOTES** Use @ISAAF in macros to verify if a function name to be referenced is actually available. @ISAAF returns the value 1 if the function is available—that is, if the needed Add-In program has already been attached; it returns 0 otherwise. Note that the @ISAAF function does not automatically recalculate when the appropriate Add-In program is finally attached.

Examples

@ISAAF("postit") returns 1, if @POSTIT is a valid function for an Add-In program that you have already attached.

@ISAAF("pv") returns 0, since @PV is a function built into 1-2-3 itself; it is not an add-in function.

See Also   These other Logical functions: @FALSE, @IF, @ISAPP, @ISERR, @ISNA, @ISNUMBER, @ISSTRING, and @TRUE.

@ISAPP

● **PURPOSE**   To test whether or not a specified program name is actually an attached 1-2-3 Add-In program.

● **SYNTAX**

@ISAPP(*name*)

where *name* is a 1-2-3 text string, formula, or reference to a cell containing a label. *Name* represents an add-in program name to be tested.

● **NOTES**   Use @ISAPP in macros to verify if an add-in program has been attached, or loaded, into memory. @ISAPP returns the value 1 if the program has already been attached; it returns 0 otherwise. Note that the @ISAPP function does not automatically recalculate when a referenced Add-In program is eventually attached.

Examples

@ISAPP("auditor") returns 1 if the AUDITOR Add-In program has been attached; it returns 0 otherwise.

See Also   These other Logical functions: @FALSE, @IF, @ISAAF, @ISERR, @ISNA, @ISNUMBER, @ISSTRING, and @TRUE.

@ISERR

- **PURPOSE** To determine if a 1-2-3 cell or expression has the value ERR.

- **SYNTAX**

  @ISERR(x)

where x is any 1-2-3 value or string quantity, single cell, or logical condition.

- **NOTES** This function tests for the unique 1-2-3 ERR value; it is not equivalent to the label "ERR". Use this function in conjunction with @IF to stop any ERR ripple-through effects in formulas that depend on cells that contain ERR. Also, use @ISERR to protect formulas from the consequences of divisions by zero.

Examples

Suppose that you are calculating engineering angles using conventional right triangle techniques. A tangent is defined by the *opposite* side divided by the *adjacent* side of the right triangle. If your calculations find the length of the opposite side in cell D1, and the length of the adjacent side in cell D2, then the desired angle can be obtained with the arc tangent function @ATAN(D1/D2).

However, in certain geometric situations, the D2 side may become very small, even equalling zero. In this case, the mathematical arc tangent should still produce a legitimate value of 90 degrees, or @PI/2 radians. Unfortunately, the division of D1 by D2 will instead produce an ERR value that will ripple through to the @ATAN(D1/D2) function.

You can use the following formula to solve this problem:

@IF(@ISERR(@ATAN(D1/D2)),@PI/2,@ATAN(D1/D2))

If D2 contained zero, then D1/D2 would produce ERR, and so would @ATAN(D1/D2). However, @ISERR(@ATAN(D1/D2)) would stop the ripple and produce a value of 1 (a logical TRUE). Consequently, the @IF function would return the value of its second argument, or @PI/2. If no ERR was noted, then @ISERR would return 0 (a logical FALSE) and @IF would return its third argument, which is simply the value of 1-2-3's arc tangent function itself, @ATAN(D1/D2).

See Also   These other Logical functions: @FALSE, @IF, @ISAAF, @ISAPP, @ISNA, @ISNUMBER, @ISSTRING, and @TRUE.

@ISNA

● **PURPOSE**   To determine if a 1-2-3 cell or expression has the value NA.

● **SYNTAX**

   @ISNA(*x*)

where *x* is any 1-2-3 value or string quantity, single cell, or logical condition.

● **NOTES**   Use @ISNA in macros to verify that all required cell contents have been entered or successfully calculated. @ISNA returns a value of 1 (TRUE) if the input argument equals the special NA value—that is, Not Available; it returns 0 (FALSE) otherwise. Only the special value NA causes @ISNA to return 1. The label "NA" is completely different from this special value.

Examples

In a budget analysis worksheet, suppose you have a series of rows for budget categories. Separate columns, one for each fiscal period, contain actual expenditures for each category. Each column entry can be initialized at the beginning of the fiscal year to @NA, to be replaced later by an actual dollar amount when it is available for the period. The column sums (using @SUM) will contain a rippled-through value of NA until all column entries have been made.

For example, if column B contains a sample fifteen category entries for Period 1, then the formula @SUM(B5..B19) in cell B21 should typically display the total expenditures for Period 1. This value may be used in a macro that computes budgetary differences between actual values and estimated values, which are stored elsewhere on the worksheet. If even one entry—say, cell B7, which is reserved for postal expenses—remains equal to NA, then the @SUM formula will likewise contain NA. @ISNA(B21) will return a value of 1 and the macro that tests this can use a macro command to control processing and display a message about the missing data.

See Also   These other Logical functions: @FALSE, @IF, @ISAAF, @ISAPP, @ISERR, @ISNUMBER, @ISSTRING, and @TRUE.

@ISNUMBER

● **PURPOSE**   To determine if a cell or 1-2-3 expression contains a numeric value.

● **SYNTAX**

@ISNUMBER(x)

where x is any 1-2-3 value or string quantity, single cell, or logical condition.

● **NOTES**   Use @ISNUMBER in macros or in worksheet cells to ensure that one or more required values have been entered correctly.

If an expected value is not numeric, this function returns a 0 (FALSE). In this instance, a special error handling macro code can be invoked, or a simple error message can be displayed.

Examples

Suppose your worksheet manages a point-of-sale cash register operation. For each item purchased, an entry is required for unit price and quantity. Formulas multiply and sum the entries to fill in line entries, tax, and total charges.

On an example row, cell B7 may contain the entered unit price and C7 may contain the entered quantity. Cell D7 will contain a formula that multiplies B7*C7 to obtain the line entry. All line entries can be added up with an @SUM formula at the bottom of column D. Meanwhile, column E can contain formulas to display an error message if any entry error is made. For example, the following simple formula in cell E7 checks for the correct entry of a numeric value for unit price in cell B7:

@IF(@ISNUMBER(B7)," ",<=== Entry Error.)

A blank space is written into cell E7 after any legitimate number is entered into B7. If any text keys are struck by accident, this formula returns an attention getting message: (<=== Entry Error.).

See Also   These other Logical functions: @FALSE, @IF, @ISAAF, @ISAPP, @ISERR, @ISNA, @ISSTRING, and @TRUE.

@ISSTRING

● **PURPOSE**   To determine if a cell or 1-2-3 expression contains a label or text string.

• SYNTAX

@ISSTRING(*x*)

where *x* is any 1-2-3 value or string quantity, single cell, or logical condition.

• NOTES   Use @ISSTRING in macros or in worksheet cells to ensure that one or more required values have been entered correctly. If an expected value is not a label or a text string, this function returns a 0 (FALSE). In this instance, special error handling macro code can be invoked, or a simple error message can be displayed.

Examples

Suppose that your worksheet application required an employee name to be entered during the preparation of a vacation advance check. Before the check is cut, a macro performs a table lookup to determine wage information. But first, the EMPLOYEE cell must be checked to validate that a text string has been entered for the name. The following macro code sequence can do this example job:

```
GETNAME  {IF @ISSTRING(EMPLOYEE)}{BRANCH OK}
         {GETLABEL "Employee's Name?",EMPLOYEE}
         {BRANCH GETNAME}
OK       {CALC}
```

If no name has yet been entered into the EMPLOYEE cell, the macro would ensure that the user was prompted to enter a name. Further processing—such as table lookup, check writing, and so on—would then continue at the OK label.

See Also   These other Logical functions: @FALSE, @IF, @ISAAF, @ISAPP, @ISERR, @ISNA, @ISNUMBER, and @TRUE.

@LEFT

- **PURPOSE**   To extract the leftmost characters in a string.

- **SYNTAX**

    @LEFT(*string,n*)

where

- *string* is any 1-2-3 text string or equivalent, and

- *n* specifies the desired number of leftmost characters.

- **NOTES**   If *n* is 0, a conventional zero-length—or *empty*—string results. If *n* specifies a number that is greater than the string length, the entire original *string* is returned.

Examples

Suppose that your 1-2-3 spreadsheet had a customer name column, with each cell containing the customer's last name and first name separated by a comma, and you wanted to construct a mail-merge macro that only required a last name. For example, suppose that cell A1 contained "Robbins, Judd", and you wanted to construct a formal letter greeting, such as "Dear Mr. Robbins." You could use @LEFT to extract the last name with this formula:

@LEFT(A1,@FIND(",",A1,0))

In this example, the number of leftmost characters to extract is itself a variable and is calculated with another function, @FIND. First, @FIND searches cell A1 to discover the location of the comma (offset 7). Since this number is offset from the zero position in the string, it can be used directly for *n* to identify how many characters (seven in this case: R-o-b-b-i-n-s) to extract from the beginning of A1, up to but not including the comma.

See Also   These other string functions: @CHAR, @CLEAN, @CODE, @EXACT, @FIND, @LENGTH, @LOWER, @MID, @N,

@PROPER, @REPEAT, @REPLACE, @RIGHT, @S, @STRING, @TRIM, @UPPER, and @VALUE.

@LENGTH

- **PURPOSE**   To determine the number of characters in a string.

- **SYNTAX**

    @LENGTH(*string*)

    where *string* is any 1-2-3 string, formula, or cell reference that evaluates to a string.

- **NOTES**   Use @LENGTH in formulas to help center text, or to control the precise number of characters to print on labels or preprinted forms.

Examples

Suppose, to prepare an overhead transparency, you wish to center a series of left-justified labels. The following formula in cell B2 would center the label from cell A2 within column B, assuming your column B is 30 characters wide:

    @REPEAT(" ",(30–@LENGTH(A2))/2)&A2

This formula first uses @LENGTH to calculate the length of the label in A2. For example, if "DISPLAY" was the label in cell A2, @LENGTH(A2) would return 7. Seven is subtracted from the total column width of 30 to obtain the number of blank spaces—23 in this case—to be divided between the left and right side of the label. Dividing 23 by two obtains the number 11.5—the number of blank spaces needed on each side to center the label. However, because 1-2-3 cannot deal in half-spaces, the truncated integer value of 11 is used and 1-2-3 inserts 11 blank spaces before the string. The @REPEAT function uses this number to repeat a blank space " " 11 times. Finally, the actual string in cell A2 is concatenated to the generated spaces, and this combination is stored in cell B2 for printing. Ideally, you should have a WYSIWYG large-presentation-style font to view the centered label onscreen.

See Also These other string functions: @CHAR, @CLEAN, @CODE, @EXACT, @FIND, @LEFT, @LOWER, @MID, @N, @PROPER, @REPEAT, @REPLACE, @RIGHT, @S, @STRING, @TRIM, @UPPER, and @VALUE.

@LN

● **PURPOSE** To calculate the natural logarithm (base *e*) of a 1-2-3 value.

● **SYNTAX**

@LN(*x*)

where *x* is any positive (greater than zero) 1-2-3 value.

Examples

If *x* equals 2.718282, then @LN(2.718282) returns 1 as its resulting value. If cell C1 contains a formula that evaluates to 10, then @LN(C1) returns 2.302585 as its result.

See Also These other mathematical functions: @ABS, @ACOS, @ASIN, @ATAN, @ATAN2, @COS, @EXP, @INT, @LOG, @MOD, @PI, @RAND, @ROUND, @SIN, @SQRT, and @TAN.

@LOG

● **PURPOSE** To calculate the common logarithm (base 10) of a 1-2-3 value.

• SYNTAX

@LOG(x)

where x is any positive (greater than zero) 1-2-3 value.

Examples

If x equals 2.718282, then @LOG(2.718282) returns 0.434294 as its resulting value. If cell C1 contains a formula that evaluates to a value of 10, then @LOG(C1) returns 1 as its result.

See Also   These other mathematical functions: @ABS, @ACOS, @ASIN, @ATAN, @ATAN2, @COS, @EXP, @INT, @LN, @MOD, @PI, @RAND, @ROUND, @SIN, @SQRT, and @TAN.

@LOWER

• PURPOSE   To convert uppercase, or capital, letters in a string to lowercase.

• SYNTAX

@LOWER(string)

where *string* is any 1-2-3 string, formula, or cell reference that evaluates to a string.

• NOTES   Use @LOWER to ensure that labels combined from different sources are consistently lowercase throughout a worksheet.

Examples

Suppose you are constructing an advertising layout for a product, and the label in cell D15 contains the string "20% DISCOUNT—ONE DAY ONLY". You could tone down the bold appearance with the @LOWER function. @LOWER(D15) results in the new string "20% discount—one day only".

See Also   These other string functions: @CHAR, @CLEAN, @CODE, @EXACT, @FIND, @LEFT, @LENGTH, @MID, @N, @PROPER, @REPEAT, @REPLACE, @RIGHT, @S, @STRING, @TRIM, @UPPER, and @VALUE.

@MAX

- **PURPOSE**   To obtain the largest value in a group of cells.

- **SYNTAX**

  @MAX(*list*)

where *list* is any series of 1-2-3 cells or range names separated by commas.

- **NOTES**   Statistical functions attempt to include a value from each cell in the specified *list* into the selected operation. If the cell does not contain a value, or a formula that evaluates to a value, 1-2-3 treats it as a zero value in determining the largest entry in the *list*. This may produce an unexpected result, since @MAX will return zero if all other numeric values are negative in the *list* range that also includes a label.

Examples

Suppose that the named cell range INVOICES contained hundreds of dollar entries for the month of June. If the largest invoice was for $2300, then @MAX(INVOICES) would return the value 2300.

See Also   These other statistical functions: @AVG, @COUNT, @MIN, @STD, @SUM, and @VAR.

@MID

● **PURPOSE** To extract a substring of characters from a specified string.

● **SYNTAX**

@MID(*string,start,n*)

where

- *string* is any 1-2-3 string expression;

- *start* is any 1-2-3 value that represents the starting offset position within *string* at which the text extraction is to begin; and

- *n* specifies how many characters to return, beginning at the *start* offset position.

● **NOTES** The name @MID originally served to extract a smaller string from the middle of a larger one. However, depending on the values for *start* and *n*, the extracted portion can begin with the first character, end with the last character, or even be the entire original string.

Examples

Suppose your worksheet contains a macro for controlling investments. It prompts the user to enter a stock exchange code, followed by a colon and the full business name of the company you're investing in. For example, to add a new investment, you might enter the following into cell A1 after being prompted by the macro:

IBM:International Business Machines

You can later use @MID, with some help from the @FIND function, to extract the Company name from the original cell entry. For example, the formula

@MID(A1,@FIND(":",A1,0)+1,35)

finds the colon symbol and adds 1 to this offset to determine the *start* offset for the actual company name. It then specifies 35 as the number of characters to extract. This results in all characters through the remainder of the cell, because 35 characters is typically the maximum number of characters allocated for company names in computer applications.

See Also   These other string functions: @CHAR, @CLEAN, @CODE, @EXACT, @FIND, @LEFT, @LENGTH, @LOWER, @N, @PROPER, @REPEAT, @REPLACE, @RIGHT, @S, @STRING, @TRIM, @UPPER, and @VALUE.

@MIN

- **PURPOSE**   To obtain the smallest value in a group of cells.

- **SYNTAX**

    @MIN(*list***)**

where *list* is any series of 1-2-3 cells or range names separated by commas.

- **NOTES**   Statistical functions attempt to include a value from each cell in the specified *list* into the selected operation. If the cell does not contain a value, or a formula that evaluates to a value, 1-2-3 treats it as a zero value in determining the largest entry in the *list*. This may produce an unexpected result, since @MIN will return zero if all other numeric values are positive in a *list* range that also includes a label.

Examples

Suppose that the named cell range SALARIES contained all employee salary figures. If your company's smallest salary was $250 per week, @MIN(SALARIES) would return the value 250.

See Also These other statistical functions: @AVG, @COUNT, @MAX, @STD, @SUM, and @VAR.

@MINUTE

• **PURPOSE** To obtain the minute value (0 to 59) from a 1-2-3 decimal time number.

• **SYNTAX**

@MINUTE(*timevalue*)

where *timevalue* is a 1-2-3 value, ranging from .000000 through .999988, representing an offset number of seconds from midnight through 11:59:59P.M.

• **NOTES** Use @MINUTE in calculations involving the number of elapsed minutes, such as scientific experiments that track the elapsed time between data samples. *Timevalue* is typically obtained from formulas involving the @NOW, @TIME, or @TIMEVALUE functions.

Examples

Suppose you began a scientific experiment at 9:02A.M. and ended it at 9:44A.M. The @TIMEVALUE function could obtain the precise time values and the @MINUTE function could obtain the integer number for the number of minutes into the hour. For example, @TIMEVALUE("9:02am") would produce a result of .376388, and @MINUTE(.376388) would produce a result of 2. @TIMEVALUE("9:44am") would result in .405555, and @MINUTE(.405555) would result in 44, which represents the number of minutes after the hour.

See Also These other date and time functions: @DATE, @DATEVALUE, @DAY, @HOUR, @MONTH, @NOW, @SECOND, @TIME, @TIMEVALUE, and @YEAR.

@MOD

● **PURPOSE** To calculate the modulus, or remainder, of the division of two numbers.

● **SYNTAX**

@MOD(x, y)

where

- x is any 1-2-3 value, and
- y is any 1-2-3 value.

● **NOTES** 1-2-3 calculates the modulus function by using the following formula:

$x - (y * @INT(x/y))$

If y is zero, @MOD returns a value of ERR.

Examples

If cell C1 contains 67 and cell C2 contains 7, then @MOD(C1,C2) results in a value of 4.

Suppose you had to determine whether a value is even or odd. You could set y equal to two in the @MOD function. A modulus of zero means that the number is evenly divisible by two and was therefore even. If @MOD(G15,2) equals zero, then the value found in cell G15 would be even.

See Also These other mathematical functions: @ABS, @ACOS, @ASIN, @ATAN, @ATAN2, @COS, @EXP, @INT, @LN, @LOG, @PI, @RAND, @ROUND, @SIN, @SQRT, and @TAN.

@MONTH

● **PURPOSE**   To obtain the month of the year for the date represented by a 1-2-3 date value.

● **SYNTAX**

@MONTH(*datenumber*)

where *datenumber* is a 1-2-3 value that ranges from an offset number of days from January 1, 1900 through December 31, 2099, and the number 1 represents 1/1/1900, and the maximum value 73050 represents 12/31/2099.

● **NOTES**   Use this function to obtain the numeric month value of a specific date for subsequent date calculations. Use it also to track or display months only for date events, such as personnel reviews that are scheduled for upcoming months.

Examples

You could use the /Data Query Extract command to determine which employees are to be reviewed by their managers in a certain month. You could set up a column of @MONTH functions, say column D, to compute the month value for the date numbers, presumably stored in column C. You could then extract all employee records for a particular month. For example, if cell B5 contained the text string "2/23/49", cell C5 might contain @DATEVALUE(B5), which would return the number 17952. Cell D5 might contain @MONTH(C5), which would then return the number 2, representing the second month (February).

See Also   These other date and time functions: @DATE, @DATEVALUE, @DAY, @HOUR, @MINUTE, @NOW, @SECOND, @TIME, @TIMEVALUE, and @YEAR.

@N

- **PURPOSE** To convert any cell (or the first cell in a range) to a numeric value.

- **SYNTAX**

  @N(*range*)

where *range* is any cell identifier or multi-cell range.

- **NOTES** Whenever you specify a single-cell argument for *range*, 1-2-3 converts the argument to a formal range.

Examples

If cell B1 contained 4, and F1 contained "Green", then @N(B1) would contain 4 and @N(F1) would contain 0. If cell range E1..G2 contained six labels, and the entire range is named COLORS, then @N(COLORS) would equal 0. Because 1-2-3 converts the argument to a formal range whenever you specify a single-cell argument, B1 would change in your formula to B1..B1 in this example.

See Also These other string functions: @CHAR, @CLEAN, @CODE, @EXACT, @FIND, @LEFT, @LENGTH, @LOWER, @MID, @PROPER, @REPEAT, @REPLACE, @RIGHT, @S, @STRING, @TRIM, @UPPER, and @VALUE.

@NA

- **PURPOSE** To produce the special cell value NA, or "Not Available."

- **SYNTAX**

  @NA

• **NOTES**   Use @NA to indicate that a cell's contents haven't been entered or are to be calculated after the user has entered data. If one cell evaluates to NA, all formulas that depend on that cell will also evaluate to NA.

NA is a unique character display that represents a special 1-2-3 value; it is not equivalent to the label "NA", which would otherwise look the same in the cell.

Examples

Suppose that a user is expected to enter a department resource code into a cell named USERCODE. In order to continue executing a macro that controls specialized departmental processing, this USERCODE is compared to a DEPTCODE cell that already exists elsewhere in the worksheet. Although an actual macro would control more extensive processing, the following formula will demonstrate @NA:

@IF(USERCODE=DEPTCODE,"Matching","Different")

For our example, you must first store @NA in the USERCODE cell. That way, NA will display until users enter something into the USERCODE cell. The formula returns "Matching" if USERCODE equals DEPTCODE, or "Different" if USERCODE does not equal DEPTCODE. However, it displays NA until an entry is made into USERCODE.

See Also   These other special functions: @?, @@, @CELL, @CELLPOINTER, @CHOOSE, @COLS, @ERR, @HLOOKUP, @INDEX, @ROWS, and @VLOOKUP.

@NOW

• **PURPOSE**   To obtain the 1-2-3 numeric value that corresponds to the current system date and time.

- **SYNTAX**

@NOW

- **NOTES** The numeric value returned by @NOW is a *floating point number*—a number with digits to either side of the decimal point. The integer portion represents the date and the decimal portion represents the time. The date (integer) portion is a 1-2-3 value that ranges from an offset number of days from January 1, 1900 through December 31, 2099. The number 1 represents 1/1/1900, and the maximum value 73050 represents 12/31/2099. The decimal portion is a 1-2-3 value, ranging from .000000 through .999988, representing an offset number of seconds from midnight through 11:59:59 P.M.

Use @NOW to time-stamp a worksheet at printing time or to calculate elapsed time for operations such as billing that calculate the number of elapsed days, or for engineering data sampling operations that calculate the amount of elapsed hours or minutes.

Examples

If the time of day is 2:43:21 P.M, and the date is July 14, 1991, then @NOW will return 33433.61343.

See Also These other date and time functions: @DATE, @DATEVALUE, @DAY, @HOUR, @MINUTE, @MONTH, @SECOND, @TIME, @TIMEVALUE, and @YEAR.

@NPV

- **PURPOSE** To compute the net present value of a non-uniform group of future cash flows.

- **SYNTAX**

@NPV(*interest,cashflows*)

where

- *interest* is a 1-2-3 value that represents a fixed periodic decimal or percentage interest rate; and

- *cashflows* is a 1-2-3 single-column or single-row range that contains the series of cash flow values.

● **NOTES** @NPV discounts the future cash flow values by the periodic *interest* rate. @NPV assumes that the cash flow values are made at equal time intervals and at the end of each time period. If a time period contains no specific cash flow amount, you must enter a zero for the cell that represents that specific time interval's contribution to the cash flows.

@NPV calculates its return value with the following formula:

$$\sum_{i=1}^{n} \frac{\text{cashflows}_i}{(1 + \text{interest})^i}$$

where *i* ranges from one to the number of cash flow values.

Examples

Suppose you were selling your house and a prospective buyer proposed that you carry back $50,000 of your asking price as a second mortgage. Specifically, he proposed to pay you $20,000 in two years, followed by $10,000 at the end of each of the succeeding three years. You wish to know what the net present value of such an offer really represents.

First, you would have to set up a range of cells, say B1..B60, to represent the CASHFLOWS values. You would need an entry for each so all cells have a zero except the payment months: B24 contains 20,000, while B36, B48, and B60 each contain 10,000. If the interest rate (10%) to use in the analysis were in a single-cell range called INTEREST, you would divide it by twelve to obtain the discount rate. @NPV(INTEREST/12,CASHFLOWS) returns a value of $36,597.79. This tells you that your prospective buyer's offer is tantamount to a $13,000 to $14,000 reduction in the offering price of your house.

See Also These other financial functions: @CTERM, @DDB, @FV, @IRR, @PMT, @PV, @RATE, @SLN, @SYD, and @TERM.

@PI

● **PURPOSE** To obtain for other computations the numeric value of the mathematical constant π.

● **SYNTAX**

@PI

● **NOTES** This function requires no arguments and is replaced during calculation with the number 3.1415926536.

Examples

To calculate the circumference (2π*r*) of a circle whose radius (*r*) is seven inches, you can use the 1-2-3 formula

2*@PI*7

This results in a value of 43.98229715.

See Also These other mathematical functions: @ABS, @ACOS, @ASIN, @ATAN, @ATAN2, @COS, @EXP, @INT, @LN, @LOG, @MOD, @RAND, @ROUND, @SIN, @SQRT, and @TAN.

@PMT

● **PURPOSE** To compute the payment required to amortize a loan at a fixed interest rate over a specified number of payment periods.

• SYNTAX

@PMT(*principal,interest,term*)

where

- *principal* is a 1-2-3 value representing the dollar amount of the loan;

- *interest* is a 1-2-3 value, expressed in decimal or percentage form, that represents the periodic interest rate; and

- *term* is a 1-2-3 value that represents the number of payment periods.

• NOTES

Use this function for amortizing a loan, or for calculating an annuity's regular payment. @PMT uses the following financial formula to calculate a payment required:

$$\text{principal} * \{\text{interest}/[(1 - (\text{interest} + 1)^{-\text{term}}]\}$$

This formula assumes that the payment is made at the end of the payment period. If you wish to make the payment at the beginning of the period (as in most annuities), you should divide the @PMT functional value by the quantity *(1 + interest)*.

Examples

Suppose that you've borrowed $200,000 (in cell B1) to buy a house. If the bank's interest rate is 11% (in cell B2) and the loan is for a conventional thirty years (360 months in cell B3), your monthly payment is obtained from

@PMT(B1,B2/12,B3)

This results in a monthly payment of $1904.65. Note that the annual interest rate in cell B2 must be divided by twelve to obtain the monthly rate, since this is the length of the actual payment period.

See Also These other financial functions: @CTERM, @DDB, @FV, @IRR, @NPV, @PV, @RATE, @SLN, @SYD, and @TERM.

@PROPER

● **PURPOSE**   To convert each word in a text string to the proper case, in which the first letter of each word in the string is capitalized.

● **SYNTAX**

@PROPER(*string*)

where *string* is any 1-2-3 string, formula, or cell reference that evaluates to a string.

● **NOTES**   Use @PROPER to give a consistent appearance to data that has been imported from more than one source, or to data that has been entered over time by more than one person.

Examples

Suppose that column D of your worksheet contained company names that were entered over a period of years. In earlier years, the data-entry person typed all names in uppercase, but now you wish all labels to appear in proper upper- and lowercase. You could use the /Worksheet Insert Column command to insert a new column E beside the old one, and the @PROPER function to convert all column D entries to proper case. If D3, for instance, contained "COMPUTER OPTIONS", then @PROPER(D3) in cell E3 would result in "Computer Options". Similar formulas could convert all column D entries to proper case in column E. You could use the /Worksheet Delete Column command to remove the old column D.

See Also   These other string functions: @CHAR, @CLEAN, @CODE, @EXACT, @FIND, @LEFT, @LENGTH, @LOWER, @MID, @N, @REPEAT, @REPLACE, @RIGHT, @S, @STRING, @TRIM, @UPPER, and @VALUE.

@PV

● **PURPOSE** To determine the present value of an investment that produces regular payments, discounted at a fixed interest rate, over a specified term. Also, to compute the maximum loan amount that you can afford, given a maximum monthly payment at a specified interest rate over a fixed term.

● **SYNTAX**

@PV(*payment,interest,term*)

where

- *payment* is a 1-2-3 value representing the dollar amount invested each period;

- *interest* is a 1-2-3 value, expressed in decimal or percentage form, that represents the periodic interest rate; and

- *term* is a 1-2-3 value that represents the number of payment periods.

● **NOTES** Use this function to compare different investments over different periods of time, at different interest rates. The present value offers a consistent point of comparison for differing investment opportunities.

The @PV function uses the following formula to return a value:

$$\text{payment} * \{[1 - (1 + \text{interest})^{-\text{term}}] / \text{interest}\}$$

This value assumes that payments are made at the end of each period. If the payment is made at the beginning of the period, as is done with annuity payments, the future value will be greater. To obtain this larger value, you should multiply the return value from the function by the quantity *(1 + interest)*.

Examples

Suppose that you can afford no more than $750 per month for a mortgage. If you can obtain a loan at 10 percent for thirty years

(360 months), the following formula will inform you that you can borrow up to $85,463.11, which is the present value of the thirty-year home investment:

@PV(750,.10/12,360)

Note that the annual 10 percent interest rate must be divided by twelve to obtain a monthly interest rate, which is the number of months in the term.

See Also   These other financial functions: @CTERM, @DDB, @FV, @IRR, @NPV, @PMT, @RATE, @SLN, @SYD, and @TERM.

@RAND

- **PURPOSE**   To compute a random number between 0 and 1.

- **SYNTAX**

    @RAND

- **NOTES**   This function requires no arguments and is replaced during each recalculation with a different number between 0 and 1. Use this to generate a statistically unbiased series of example numbers for selections or simulations.

Once you are satisfied with your random number generations, you can retain the randomly generated numbers by applying the /Range Value command to the cells containing the @RAND formulas. If you do not do this, each subsequent worksheet recalculation will compute a new series of random numbers.

Examples

To generate a series of random numbers between 0 and 34, use the following formula in a range of cells:

@INT(@RAND*35)

To generate a series of random numbers between 1 and 10, use the following formula in a range of cells:

1+@INT(@RAND*10)

See Also   /Range Value, and these other mathematical functions: @ABS, @ACOS, @ASIN, @ATAN, @ATAN2, @COS, @EXP, @INT, @LN, @LOG, @MOD, @PI, @ROUND, @SIN, @SQRT, and @TAN.

@RATE

● **PURPOSE**   To compute the fixed interest rate required for a current investment to grow to a specified future amount over a specific number of compounding terms.

● **SYNTAX**

@RATE(*futurevalue,presentvalue,term*)

where

- *futurevalue* is a 1-2-3 value that represents the desired eventual value of the accumulating investment,

- *presentvalue* is a 1-2-3 value that represents the current value of an investment, and

- *term* is a 1-2-3 value representing the number of compounding periods.

● **NOTES**   Use @RATE for investment analyses or comparisons. @RATE uses the following formula to calculate its result:

$$(fv/pv)^{(1/term)} - 1$$

where *fv* is the *futurevalue* and *pv* is the *presentvalue*.

Examples

Suppose that you've sold a piece of property and netted $100,000. You plan to invest this money for eventual payment of your children's college expenses. Calculating your future needs to be $200,000 in six years, you want to know what interest rate will be required to make this a reality. The following formula will calculate this amount for you:

@RATE(200000,100000,72)

This formula results in a 0.97 percent monthly rate. To convert this accurately to an annual rate, you must use the following adjustment formula:

$(1+@RATE\ (200000,100000,72))^{12}-1$

which results in an annual interest rate of 12.25 percent.

See Also   These other financial functions: @CTERM, @DDB, @FV, @IRR, @NPV, @PMT, @PV, @SLN, @SYD, and @TERM.

@REPEAT

● **PURPOSE**   To generate a repeated series of the same character, given the number of repetitions.

● **SYNTAX**

@REPEAT(*string,n*)

where

- *string* is any 1-2-3 string, formula, or cell reference that evaluates to a string; and

- *n* is a positive integer, formula, or cell reference that evaluates to an integer.

● **NOTES** Use @REPEAT in formulas to help center text, and to duplicate special characters, such as spaces, asterisks, or graphic symbols, in printouts or presentations.

Examples

Suppose you are preparing an overhead transparency and you wish to center a series of currently left-justified labels. The following formula in cell B2 would center the label from cell A2 within the presumed thirty-character-wide column B:

@REPEAT(" ",(30–@LENGTH(A2))/2)&A2

This formula first uses @LENGTH to calculate the length of the label in A2. In the example below, the length of the "DISPLAY" label in cell A2 is 7. This value is subtracted from the column width of 30 to obtain the number of blank spaces—23 in this case—to be divided between the left and right side of the label. Dividing 23 by two obtains the number 11.5—the number of blank spaces needed on each side to center the label. However, because 1-2-3 cannot deal in half-spaces, the truncated integer value of 11 is used and 1-2-3 inserts 11 spaces before the string. The @REPEAT function uses this number to repeat a blank space (" ") 11 times. Finally, the actual string in cell A2 is concatenated to the generated spaces, and this combination is stored in cell B2. In Table III.2, the presentation topics appear in column A, and the formula results appear in column B.

Table III.2: Results of Using @REPEAT to Center Labels

	A	B
1		
2	DISPLAY	DISPLAY
3	FORMATTING	FORMATTING
4	GRAPHING	GRAPHING
5	STYLES	STYLES
6	PRINTING	PRINTING

See Also   These other string functions: @CHAR, @CLEAN, @CODE, @EXACT, @FIND, @LEFT, @LENGTH, @LOWER, @MID, @N, @PROPER, @REPLACE, @RIGHT, @S, @STRING, @TRIM, @UPPER, and @VALUE.

@REPLACE

● **PURPOSE**   To replace a portion of one string with another string.

● **SYNTAX**

   @REPLACE(*original,start,n,new*)

where

   • *original* is the string that is to be partially changed;

   • *start* is the offset position, beginning with 0, at which to begin the replacement process;

   • *n* is the number of characters in the original string to take away; and

   • *new* is the updating text that is to replace *n* characters in the *original* string.

● **NOTES**   If the number of *new* characters exceeds the number *n* of *original* characters that are to be replaced, the *original* string is simply widened to make room for the *new* characters after *n* characters in the original string are removed.

You can use this function to append a *new* string to the *original* string by simply setting the *start* value to a number that is larger than the length of the *original* string.

Examples

Suppose you had to update a telephone number because the area code changed from 617 to 508. If cell A1 contained "617-524-4099", then @REPLACE(A1,0,3,"508") would return the updated text string "508-524-4099". Three characters are replaced, beginning with the zero position.

Suppose that your database contained an entire column of such phone numbers. You could create a parallel column of formulas, such as the following:

@IF(@LEFT(A1,3)="617",@REPLACE(A1,0,3,"508"),A1)

Each cell, such as A1 in our example, that contained a phone number beginning with "617" would be updated to include the new area code 508. The @REPLACE function would return the updated string only if the @LEFT function discovered that the first three characters were "617". All other phone numbers would make the @LEFT function return a FALSE result. Consequently, the @IF function would return the original string from A1—the third @IF argument—instead of the @REPLACE functional result—the second @IF argument.

See Also   These other string functions: @CHAR, @CLEAN, @CODE, @EXACT, @FIND, @LEFT, @LENGTH, @LOWER, @MID, @N, @PROPER, @REPEAT, @RIGHT, @S, @STRING, @TRIM, @UPPER, and @VALUE.

@RIGHT

- **PURPOSE**   To extract the rightmost characters in a string.

- **SYNTAX**

  @RIGHT(*string,n*)

where

- *string* is any 1-2-3 text string or equivalent, and

- *n* specifies the desired number of rightmost characters.

● **NOTES**   If *n* is 0, a conventional zero length, or empty, string results. If *n* specifies a number that is greater than the string length, the entire original *string* is returned. If the target *string* contains any trailing blank spaces, consider using the @TRIM function to extract these characters first.

Examples

Suppose your 1-2-3 spreadsheet contained a column of customer names, but each cell contained the customer's last name and first name, separated by a comma. You could construct a mail-merge macro to produce a last name only. For example, suppose that cell A3 contained "Robbins, Judd", but you wanted to construct a personalized letter that began "Dear Judd." You could use @RIGHT to extract the first name with this formula:

@RIGHT(A3,@LENGTH(A3)−@FIND(" ",A3,0)−1)

This formula returns the four characters "Judd" from the string in cell A3. In this example, the number of rightmost characters to extract is itself a variable and is calculated by two other functions, @LENGTH and @FIND. First, the total length (13 characters) of the string in cell A3 is obtained with @LENGTH. Then @FIND searches cell A3 to discover the location of the blank space—at offset 8—that follows the comma punctuation. Since this number is an offset from the zero position in the string, the formula must then subtract one to ensure that the rightmost number *n* of characters (13 − 8 − 1, or 4) obtained by @RIGHT does not begin with the space separator character itself.

See Also   These other string functions: @CHAR, @CLEAN, @CODE, @EXACT, @FIND, @LEFT, @LENGTH, @LOWER, @MID, @N, @PROPER, @REPEAT, @REPLACE, @S, @STRING, @TRIM, @UPPER, and @VALUE.

@ROUND

● **PURPOSE**   To round off a value to a specified number of decimal places.

● SYNTAX

@ROUND(*x,n*)

where

- *x* is any 1-2-3 value, and
- *n* is a value in the range −15 to +15.

● NOTES If *n* is positive, the value of *x* is rounded to that many decimal places to the right of the decimal point. If *n* is negative, the value of *x* is rounded to that many decimal places to the left of the decimal point.

If *n* is not itself an integer, then *n* is first truncated and its integer portion is used in the rounding calculation.

Examples

@ROUND(17.854, 1) results in a value of 17.9; @ROUND(−244.86, 0) results in a value of −245; and @ROUND(1234.876,−2) results in 1200.

See Also These other mathematical functions: @ABS, @ACOS, @ASIN, @ATAN, @ATAN2, @COS, @EXP, @INT, @LN, @LOG, @MOD, @PI, @RAND, @SIN, @SQRT, and @TAN.

@ROWS

● PURPOSE To determine the number of rows in a range of cells.

● SYNTAX

@ROWS(*range*)

where *range* is any 1-2-3 range name or address.

● **NOTES**   Use this function in macros to determine how many currently existing rows in a changing range should be processed.

Examples

Suppose your ongoing budget analysis used the actual expenditures stored in a range called ACTUALS. This range can span a number of rows, ranging from 1 to however many budgeting categories are currently being tracked. If you've entered four months of data for seven categories of expenditure, and ACTUALS now spans B4..E10—in other words, seven budgeting categories in rows 4 to 10, and four months in columns B to E—the function @ROWS(ACTUALS) would return a value of 7. This value could then be used by an automated macro to repeat some printing or analysis logic this variable (seven) number of times.

See Also   These other special functions: @?, @@, @CELL, @CELLPOINTER, @CHOOSE, @COLS, @ERR, @HLOOKUP, @INDEX, @NA, and @VLOOKUP.

@S

● **PURPOSE**   To convert any cell (or the first cell in a range) to a string quantity.

● **SYNTAX**

   @S(*range*)

where *range* is any cell identifier or multi-cell range.

● **NOTES**   If the specified cell, or first cell in a range, contains a label, @S returns that label. If the cell contains a value, 1-2-3 replaces it with an empty string.

Use this function to quickly determine which labels that begin with digits have been erroneously entered as numbers.

Examples

Suppose column D in your database is six characters wide and contains five-digit ZIP codes (one character is reserved to separate columns). If a ZIP code was entered without a label prefix, it would look the same as the other ZIP codes on the screen, but 1-2-3 would consider it a number. Later string manipulations might fail because of ERR calculations between strings and values.

In particular, suppose cell D4 contained the value 94530, rather than the label "94530". If you used column E to convert this and all other ZIP codes, the formula @S(D4) in cell E4 would display as a blank cell, calling attention to the input error.

See Also   These other string functions: @CHAR, @CLEAN, @CODE, @EXACT, @FIND, @LEFT, @LENGTH, @LOWER, @MID, @N, @PROPER, @REPEAT, @REPLACE, @RIGHT, @STRING, @TRIM, @UPPER, and @VALUE.

@SECOND

● **PURPOSE**   To obtain the seconds value (0 to 59) from a 1-2-3 decimal time number.

● **SYNTAX**

@SECOND(*timevalue*)

where *timevalue* is a 1-2-3 value, ranging from .000000 through .999988, representing an offset number of seconds from midnight through 11:59:59P.M.

● **NOTES**   Use @SECOND in calculations involving the number of elapsed seconds, such as scientific experiments that must track the elapsed time between data samples. *Timevalue* is typically obtained from formulas involving the @NOW, @TIME, or @TIME-VALUE functions.

Examples

Suppose that you begin a scientific experiment at 9:02:15A.M. and end it at 9:02:52A.M. The @TIMEVALUE function could obtain the precise time values. The @SECOND function could then obtain the integer number for the number of seconds into the minute. For example, @TIMEVALUE("9:02:15am") results in .376562, and @SECOND(.376562) results in 15. @TIMEVALUE("9:02:52am") results in .376990, and @SECOND(.376990) results in 52, which represents the number of seconds into the minute.

See Also These other date and time functions: @DATE, @DATEVALUE, @DAY, @HOUR, @MINUTE, @MONTH, @NOW, @TIME, @TIMEVALUE, and @YEAR.

@SIN

● **PURPOSE** To calculate the sine of an angle.

● **SYNTAX**

@SIN(*x*)

where *x* is a 1-2-3 value representing the angle in radians.

● **NOTES** X can have any value. Remember that there are 2 π radians in 360 degrees. You can convert from degrees to the necessary angle in radians by using the @PI function

Angle in Radians = @PI/180 * Angle in Degrees

The @SIN function returns a sine value from −1 to +1.

Examples

If *x* equals 30 degrees, you can first convert that to radians by multiplying 30 times @PI and dividing by 180. This returns 0.523598. The @SIN(0.523598) function returns the expected value of 0.5.

If cell B1 contains an angle in degrees of 60, the formula

@PI/180*B1

in cell B2 would result in 1.047197. A final formula in cell B3 of @SIN(B2) would produce the sine of 60 degrees, or 0.866025.

See Also These other mathematical functions: @ABS, @ACOS, @ASIN, @ATAN, @ATAN2, @COS, @EXP, @INT, @LN, @LOG, @MOD, @PI, @RAND, @ROUND, @SQRT, and @TAN.

@SLN

● **PURPOSE** To compute the straight line depreciation allowance of an asset.

● **SYNTAX**

@SLN(*startvalue,endvalue,life*)

where

- *startvalue* is a 1-2-3 value that represents the initial cost of the asset,

- *endvalue* is a 1-2-3 value that represents the estimated salvage value of the asset at the end of its useful life, and

- *life* is the number of periods the asset takes to depreciate from *startvalue* to *endvalue*.

● **NOTES** @SLN calculates an equal depreciation allowance for each period in the useful life of the asset. @SLN uses the following simple formula, which divides the depreciable, or loss in, value by the number of depreciation periods:

(startvalue – endvalue) / life

Examples

Suppose that you've bought an office copier for $25,000. You assume from experience that you will replace it in five years, and that you will be able to resell it then for $10,000. The annual depreciation allowance for the five years of use is obtained as @SLN(25000,10000,5), or $3000.

See Also   These other financial functions: @CTERM, @DDB, @FV, @IRR, @NPV, @PMT, @PV, @RATE, @SYD, and @TERM.

@SQRT

- **PURPOSE**   To calculate the positive square root of a value.

- **SYNTAX**

  @SQRT(x)

where x is any 1-2-3 value.

- **NOTES** X must be zero or positive. Attempting to calculate the square root of a negative number will result in a 1-2-3 value of ERR.

Examples

The quadratic equation is a familiar sight to engineers and scientists. In order not to confuse the unknown variable with the argument of this function, I'll use z in the equation:

$$az^2 + bz + c = 0$$

The solution of this equation for z is :

$$\frac{-b \pm \sqrt{(b^2 - 4ac)}}{2a}$$

If you are solving the specific equation

$$z^2 + 5z - 14 = 0$$

then a=1, b=5, and c=−14. If these three values are stored in cells E5, E6, and E7, then the following 1-2-3 formula will produce the first root of +2:

(−E6+@SQRT(E6∗E6−4∗E5∗E7))/(2∗E5)

See Also   These other mathematical functions: @ABS, @ACOS, @ASIN, @ATAN, @ATAN2, @COS, @EXP, @INT, @LN, @LOG, @MOD, @PI, @RAND, @ROUND, @SIN, and @TAN.

@STD

● **PURPOSE**   To calculate the standard deviation of a group of 1-2-3 cells.

● **SYNTAX**

@STD(*list*)

where *list* is any series of 1-2-3 cells or range names separated by commas.

● **NOTES**   The @STD function computes the variance of a group of values from the average value. If the individual values are close to the average, the group will have a small standard deviation. If one or more values differ markedly from the average, the standard deviation will be high.

1-2-3 uses the population method to compute standard deviation, which assumes that *list* includes the entire population:

$$\text{Standard Deviation} = \sqrt{\frac{\sum (l_i - m)^2}{n}}$$

where l_i is the ith entry value from the *list*

m is the mean, or average, of the *list*

n is the number of elements in the *list*

Be careful when you include cell names and ranges in your *list*. Statistical functions attempt to include into the selected operation a value from each cell in the specified *list*. With one exception, which is noted below, the @STD function will ignore any contribution from cells that are truly empty of data contents or formatting information. However, if *list* contains any of the following types of cells, each will contribute a zero value to the computation and skew the computed standard deviation:

- cells containing labels;

- cells containing a label prefix only, which seem empty but really are not;

- cells containing spaces; and

- blank cells that are explicitly included by name.

Examples

Suppose that cell A6 is blank, while cells A1..A5 contain the test scores 85, 65, 70, 75, and 95. In this case, @STD(A1..A5) would return a value of 10.77032, which represents the variance from the average of the five scores. @STD(A1..A6) would similarly return a value of 10.77032 because the blank cell A6 would not be included in the calculations.

However, @STD(A1..A5,A6) would produce an incorrect and highly skewed standard deviation value of 30.68658, because here you explicitly included cell A6 by name. This adds a spurious value of zero to the population data being used.

See Also   @DSTD, and these other statistical functions: @AVG, @COUNT, @MAX, @MIN, @SUM, and @VAR.

@STRING

- **PURPOSE**   To convert a numeric value to a text string.

- **SYNTAX**

  @STRING(*number,decimals*)

where

- *number* is any 1-2-3 value, and

- *decimals* is the number of desired decimal places to appear in the resulting string quantity.

- **NOTES**   Use this function when concatenating information for display or printing that involves a combination of cells containing both text and numeric values. Note, in the examples below, that the dollar sign is incorporated into the final result by explicit character reference. This is necessary because the value converted by @STRING ignores any formatting. So even if cell G15 in the example was formatted to appear as a dollars-and-cents quantity, the @STRING function would only convert the G15 value to show digits and a decimal point.

Examples

Suppose that cell G15 contained a current account balance of 455 during the preparation of a billing invoice. If cell A3 contained the label "Current Balance is", you could construct a text string for printing that combines this label and the G15 value by using this formula:

+A3&" = $"&@STRING(G15,2)

This would produce the concatenated result

Current Balance is = $455.00

Notice how the result combines the label from A3 with a text string consisting of a blank space, an equal sign, another blank space, and a dollar sign, and that the G15 value is converted to a text string with two decimal places.

See Also   These other string functions: @CHAR, @CLEAN, @CODE, @EXACT, @FIND, @LEFT, @LENGTH, @LOWER, @MID, @N, @PROPER, @REPEAT, @REPLACE, @RIGHT, @S, @TRIM, @UPPER, and @VALUE.

@SUM

- **PURPOSE**   To add up the numeric values in a group of cells.

- **SYNTAX**

   @SUM(*list*)

where *list* is any series of 1-2-3 cells or range names separated by commas.

- **NOTES**   Statistical functions attempt to include into the selected operation a value from each cell in the specified *list*. If the cell does not contain a value, or a formula that evaluates to a value, 1-2-3 treats it as a zero contribution to the total sum.

Examples

Suppose that cell A4 is blank, cell A5 contains a label, and cells A1..A3 contain the values 10, 20, and 30. In this case, @SUM(A1..A5) would return a value of 60, which is the sum of the three numeric cells (10+20+30=60) plus zero contributions from the blank and label cells.

See Also   These other statistical functions: @AVG, @COUNT, @MAX, @MIN, @STD, and @VAR.

@SYD

● **PURPOSE** To compute the accelerated depreciation allowance of an asset, using the sum-of-the-years'-digits method.

● **SYNTAX**

@SYD(*startvalue,endvalue,life,period*)

where

- *startvalue* is a 1-2-3 value that represents the initial cost of the asset,

- *endvalue* is a 1-2-3 value that represents the estimated salvage value of the asset at the end of its useful life,

- *life* is the number of periods the asset takes to depreciate from *initialvalue* to *endvalue*, and

- *period* is the specific time period for which to calculate the sum-of-the-years'-digits depreciation allowance.

● **NOTES** Use this function when you wish to reduce tax liability by a greater amount in the early years of your asset's life. Depreciation allowance is greater during the earlier periods of your asset's life. @SYD uses the following formula to calculate depreciation:

[(startvalue – endvalue)] * (life – period + 1)] / [(life * (life + 1)/2)]

Examples

Suppose that you've bought an office copier for $25,000. You assume from experience that you will replace it in five years, and that you will be able to resell it then for $10,000. You need greater tax write-offs this year because of extra income, so you use the @SYD function to calculate the first year's depreciation allowance as @SYD(25000,10000,5,1), or $5000. Repeating this formula for year's 2 through 5—changing only the last argument value—shows the reducing depreciation amounts of $4000, $3000, $2000, and $1000, all of which add up to a total depreciation allowance of $15,000.

See Also   These other financial functions: @CTERM, @DDB, @FV, @IRR, @NPV, @PMT, @PV, @RATE, @SLN, and @TERM.

@TAN

● **PURPOSE**   To calculate the tangent of an angle.

● **SYNTAX**

@TAN(x)

where x is a 1-2-3 value representing the angle in radians.

● **NOTES**   X can have any value. Remember that there are 2 π radians in 360 degrees. You can convert from degrees to the necessary angle in radians by using the @PI function

Angle in Radians = @PI/180 * Angle in Degrees

The @TAN function returns a tangent value from 0 to a very large number that can be stored and displayed, but not the mathematical value of infinity (∞), which is the true value of a ninety degree tangent.

Examples

If x equals 60 degrees, you can first convert that to radians by multiplying 60 times @pi and dividing by 180. This returns 1.047197. The @TAN(1.047197) function returns the expected value of 1.732050, or the square root of 3.

If cell B1 contains an angle in degrees of 30, the following formula in cell B2

@PI/180*B1

would result in 0.523598. A final formula in cell B3 of @TAN(B2) would produce the tangent of 30 degrees, or 0.577350.

See Also   These other mathematical functions: @ABS, @ACOS, @ASIN, @ATAN, @ATAN2, @COS, @EXP, @INT, @LN, @LOG, @MOD, @PI, @RAND, @ROUND, @SIN, and @SQRT.

@TERM

● **PURPOSE**   To calculate the compounding term—that is, the number of compounding periods—required for a series of regular investment payments to accumulate to a specified amount, given a fixed rate of interest per compounding period.

● **SYNTAX**

@TERM(*payment,interest,futurevalue*)

where

- *payment* is a 1-2-3 value representing the dollar amount invested each period;

- *interest* is a 1-2-3 value, expressed in decimal or percentage form, that represents the periodic interest rate; and

- *futurevalue* is a 1-2-3 value that represents the desired eventual value of the accumulating investment.

● **NOTES**   Remember to enter the *interest* rate for each compounding period, rather than simply for the commonly expressed annual percentage rate. The value of *interest* must be numerically greater than –1.

Examples

Suppose that you set up a payroll deduction plan with your employer, saving $200 monthly for an eventual down payment on a home. You figure that you'll need $10,000 for your down payment, and you wonder how long it will take for the monthly payroll deductions to increase at 7% annual interest to the desired $10,000.

At a 7% annual rate, the monthly—or the compounding period—interest is .07/12, so the formula to use is

@TERM(200,.07/12,10000)

This tells you that the necessary number of compounding periods is 44. Dividing 44 by twelve produces a more meaningful answer of 3²/3 years required to save enough for the down payment on the house.

See Also   These other financial functions: @CTERM, @DDB, @FV, @IRR, @NPV, @PMT, @PV, @RATE, @SLN, and @SYD.

@TIME

● **PURPOSE**   To calculate the 1-2-3 time value for a specific time of day, given three integers which represent the hour, minute, and second.

● **SYNTAX**

@TIME(*hours,minutes,seconds*)

where

- *hours* is a 1-2-3 value, ranging from 0 through 23, which represents the hour of the day from midnight through 11:00P.M;

- *minutes* is a 1-2-3 value, ranging from 0 through 59, which represents the number of minutes within an hour; and

- *seconds* is a 1-2-3 value, ranging from 0 through 59, which represents the number of seconds within a minute.

● **NOTES**   Use @TIME to obtain a 1-2-3 time value based on more recognizable hour, minute, and second quantities. A 1-2-3 time value ranges from .000000 through .999988, representing an offset number of seconds from midnight through 11:59:59P.M.

You must use 1-2-3 time values in formulas that perform time arithmetic. The value returned by @TIME is a decimal number. You must use /Range Format if you want this value to actually appear as a recognizable time on your worksheet.

Examples

Suppose that you are a lawyer and that you track your phone conversations with a 1-2-3 worksheet. You begin a call at 10:10A.M., or @TIME(10,10,0), and end it at 10:50A.M., or @TIME(10,50,0). Subtract one from the other, and you get the fractional portion of the day consumed by the call: @TIME(10,50,0) – @TIME(10,10,0) equals .451388 – .423611, or 0.027777. Multiply this value by your hourly charge, say $210 per hour, and then by 24, the number of hours per day, to obtain the final billing amount: .027777 * 210 * 24, or 140. Remember to use /Range Format to make the 140 appear as a dollar amount, such as $140.00.

See Also   These other date and time functions: @DATE, @DATEVALUE, @DAY, @HOUR, @MINUTE, @MONTH, @NOW, @SECOND, @TIMEVALUE, and @YEAR.

@TIMEVALUE

● **PURPOSE**   To calculate the 1-2-3 time value corresponding to a time expressed as a text string.

● **SYNTAX**

   @TIMEVALUE(*string*)

where *string* is a text string, formula, or cell identifier that contains a text string or formula that looks like one of the allowable 1-2-3 time formats.

● **NOTES**   *String* must be expressed in one of the four allowable formats shown in the /Range Format Date Time command. Use this function when you import text data from other programs, or when you wish to convert text strings found in other cells for the purposes of time arithmetic.

The value returned by @TIMEVALUE is a decimal number. You must use /Range Format if you wish this value to actually appear as a time on your worksheet.

Examples

Suppose that you are a lawyer and that you track your phone conversations with a 1-2-3 worksheet. You begin a call at 10:10A.M. and end it at 10:50A.M., and you wish 1-2-3 to figure out your billing after you've simply typed text strings for each of these two times. Suppose that you type "10:10am" into B3, and "10:50am" into B4. You can calculate the starting and ending time values in C3 and C4 with the formulas @TIMEVALUE(B3) and @TIMEVALUE(B4). Subtract these two time values from one another, and you obtain the fractional portion of the day consumed by the call: @TIMEVALUE("10:50am") − @TIMEVALUE ("10:10am") equals .451388 − .423611, or 0.027777. Multiply this value by your hourly charge, say $210 per hour, and then by 24, the number of hours per day, to obtain the final billing amount: .027777 ∗ 210 ∗ 24, or 140. Remember to use /Range Format to make the 140 appear as a dollar amount, such as $140.00.

See Also   These other date and time functions: @DATE, @DATEVALUE, @DAY, @HOUR, @MINUTE, @MONTH, @NOW, @SECOND, @TIME, and @YEAR.

@TRIM

- **PURPOSE**   To remove all leading, trailing, and extra consecutive blank characters from a string.

- **SYNTAX**

    @TRIM(*string*)

where *string* is any 1-2-3 string, formula, or cell reference that evaluates to a string.

● **NOTES** This function is most useful when dealing with data imported from other software programs with the /File Import command.

Examples

Suppose that you've imported an entire database from dBASE IV, or another database management program, and many cells now contain text strings with trailing blank spaces. You could remove these trailing blanks, and any excess separation blank spaces as well, by creating new columns to eventually replace the old ones. Each cell in a new parallel column would contain a formula to trim its neighbor. For example, suppose column A brought into 1-2-3 a twelve-character phone number with three trailing blank space characters, such as "415-525-5033", because the dBASE IV database field was fifteen characters wide. @LENGTH(A1) would reveal a cell data string of 15 characters. A formula @TRIM(A1) would strip off the trailing three blank spaces. @LENGTH(@TRIM(A1)) would result in a value of twelve.

See Also /File Import, and these other string functions: @CHAR, @CLEAN, @CODE, @EXACT, @FIND, @LEFT, @LENGTH, @LOWER, @MID, @N, @PROPER, @REPEAT, @REPLACE, @RIGHT, @S, @STRING, @UPPER, and @VALUE.

@TRUE

● **PURPOSE** To return a logical value of TRUE, which is equivalent to 1-2-3's numeric value of 1.

● **SYNTAX**

@TRUE

Examples

Suppose that some other worksheet cell with a range named EXCES-
SIVE tests whether or not cell A1 contains a value greater than 350:

@IF(A1>350,@TRUE,@FALSE)

This results in range EXCESSIVE containing the number 1 (logical
value TRUE) if A1 contains 350 or greater; or the number 0 (logical value FALSE) if A1 equals 350 or less. Elsewhere on your worksheet, you have a formula that tests this range EXCESSIVE:

@IF(EXCESSIVE=@TRUE,"REENTER DATA"," ")

Because you've used a test involving @TRUE, rather than an
equivalent test for 1, the processing logic is easier to read and understand. If the data entry exceeds the guideline, the prompt
"REENTER DATA" appears; other macro controlled processing
could then return the cell pointer to cell A1 for the actual data
reentry.

See Also   These other Logical functions: @FALSE, @IF, @ISAAF,
@ISAPP, @ISERR, @ISNA, @ISNUMBER, and @ISSTRING.

@UPPER

- **PURPOSE**   To convert lowercase letters in a string to uppercase.

- **SYNTAX**

  ### @UPPER(*string*)

  where *string* is any 1-2-3 string, formula, or cell reference that
  evaluates to a string.

- **NOTES**   Use @UPPER to ensure that labels combined from different sources are consistently uppercase throughout a worksheet.

Examples

Suppose that you are constructing an advertising layout for a product and the label in cell D15 contains the string "20% discount—one day only". You can embolden the overall appearance with the @UPPER function. @UPPER(D15) results in the new string "20% DISCOUNT—ONE DAY ONLY".

See Also   These other string functions: @CHAR, @CLEAN, @CODE, @EXACT, @FIND, @LEFT, @LENGTH, @LOWER, @MID, @N, @PROPER, @REPEAT, @REPLACE, @RIGHT, @S, @STRING, @TRIM, and @VALUE.

@VALUE

● **PURPOSE**   To convert a text string that looks like a number to an actual 1-2-3 value.

● **SYNTAX**

@VALUE(*string*)

where *string* is any 1-2-3 string, formula, or cell reference that evaluates to a string.

● **NOTES**   Use this function to convert labels that were entered originally as strings, but which now must be used in calculations. @VALUE is most often used when importing data from other software with the /File Import command. Sometimes, numeric values from the other software are written to text or print files as a string of characters. To be used computationally by 1-2-3, they must be converted back to numeric values.

Examples

Suppose that column G contains current account balances imported from your database program. These strings look like "125.50", "245.45", "130.00", and so on. If G2 contains "245.45", then

@VALUE(G2) produces the numeric value 245.45, which can then be used in any 1-2-3 calculation.

If cell G3 contains "130.00", then @VALUE(G3) produces the numeric value 130, which in General format does not display the numerically meaningless decimal point and the following two zeros.

See Also   /File Import, and these other string functions: @CHAR, @CLEAN, @CODE, @EXACT, @FIND, @LEFT, @LENGTH, @LOWER, @MID, @N, @PROPER, @REPEAT, @REPLACE, @RIGHT, @S, @STRING, @TRIM, and @UPPER.

@VAR

● **PURPOSE**   To compute the statistical variance of a population of values.

● **SYNTAX**

  @VAR(*list*)

where *list* is any series of 1-2-3 cells or range names separated by commas.

● **NOTES**   Like the standard deviation computation, 1-2-3 uses the population method to compute variance, which assumes that *list* includes the entire population:

$$\text{Variance=Standard Deviation Squared=} \frac{\sum (l_i - m)^2}{n}$$

where l_i is the ith entry value from the *list*

   m is the mean, or average, of the *list*

   n is the number of elements in the *list*

Be careful when you include cell names and ranges in your *list*. Statistical functions attempt to include in the selected operation a value from each cell in the specified *list*. With one exception, which is noted below, the @VAR function ignores any contribution from cells that are truly empty of data contents or formatting information. However, if *list* contains any of the following types of cells, each cell will contribute a zero value to the computation and skew the computed variance:

- cells containing labels;

- cells containing a label prefix only, which seem empty but really are not;

- cells containing spaces; and

- blank cells that are explicitly included by name.

Examples

Suppose that cell A6 is blank, while cells A1..A5 contain the test scores 85, 65, 70, 75, and 95. In this case, @VAR(A1..A5) would return a value of 116, which represents the variance for the five scores. @VAR(A1..A6) would similarly return a value of 116 because the blank cell A6 would not be included in the calculations. However, @VAR(A1..A5,A6) would produce an incorrect variance value of approximately 941.667, because here you have explicitly included cell A6 by name. This adds a spurious value of zero to the population data being used.

See Also   @DVAR, and these other statistical functions: @AVG, @COUNT, @MAX, @MIN, @STD, and @SUM.

@VLOOKUP

- **PURPOSE**   To obtain the contents of a cell from a table, given a row selector and a column selector.

• SYNTAX

@VLOOKUP(*row,range,column*)

where

- *row* is a value or string to be used to determine which row of the table to select from.

- *range* is the total extent of the 1-2-3 cell range that constitutes the table. The first column of the table contains the row data against which the *row* argument will be compared.

- *column* contains the column offset value to be used to look up an entry in the table. Column 0 is the index column, making columns 1, 2, 3 and so on the actual data columns in the table.

• NOTES   Use @VLOOKUP when you wish to look up an entry in a table based on a specifically known value or label.

The *row* selector can be any 1-2-3 quantity that evaluates to a value or a string. @VLOOKUP compares the *row* selector data against the entries in the first column of the table *range*. These entries must be in ascending order. If the *row* entry contains a text string, @VLOOKUP will expect to find that precise string in the first column of the table *range*. If the *row* entry is a value, @VLOOKUP chooses the row that begins with that value, or with the value just below the *row* value specified.

Remember that the *column* argument is an offset number for determining which column is to be used from the table.

Examples

Look at Figure III.3. The cell *range* D4..G14 is named RATES and represents a sample table of shipping rates for three example zones. After entering the weight of a package in cell B5, and the destination zone in cell B6, the following formula from cell B9 finds the shipping charges to be added to a customer's bill:

@VLOOKUP(B5,RATES,B6)

The appropriate row is found by comparing the entry in cell B5, 5 in this case. The appropriate row offset, 2, is found directly with the

Figure III.3: The vertical lookup function

zone number found in cell B6. The @VLOOKUP function returns the entry 154, found at the intersection of the specified *column* and *row* arguments.

See Also   The table lookup functions @CHOOSE, @HLOOKUP, and @INDEX, and these other special functions: @?, @@, @CELL, @CELLPOINTER, @COLS, @ERR, @NA, and @ROWS.

@YEAR

- **PURPOSE**   To obtain the numeric year for the date represented by a 1-2-3 date value.

- **SYNTAX**

    @YEAR(*datenumber*)

where *datenumber* is a 1-2-3 value that ranges from an offset number of days from January 1, 1900 through December 31, 2099. The number

1 represents 1/1/1900 and the maximum value 73050 represents 12/31/2099.

● **NOTES**   Use @YEAR in calculations that require a year only, such as employee benefit analyses based on year of hire. You can add the base year 1900 to the @YEAR value in order to obtain and display a four-digit year.

● **EXAMPLES**   If cell B2 calculates a date value for "6/15/91", then the formula 1900+@YEAR(B2) returns the four-digit year 1991.

See Also   These other date and time functions: @DATE, @DATE-VALUE, @DAY, @HOUR, @MINUTE, @MONTH, @NOW, @SECOND, @TIME, and @TIMEVALUE.

Glossary of Macro Keywords

The Glossary in this Appendix briefly explains all 1-2-3 macro instructions and their required syntax. In the Glossary, syntactical elements enclosed in square brackets are optional. You will find explanations of the older /X macro instructions at the end of the Appendix. These have been included to help you make your current version of 1-2-3 compatible with older versions of the program.

When you enter macro instructions in your worksheet, remember that you must enter them as labels. If a cell does not begin with the typical macro's open curly bracket ({), you must include a label prefix to tell 1-2-3 to treat the macro instructions as label text.

MACRO KEYWORD DEFINITIONS

{?}   Pauses a macro for user action, such as entering data or moving the cell pointer. Pressing ↵ continues to execute the macro.

~(tilde)   Simulates a ↵ key press.

{(open curly bracket)   Enables the special macro character (the open curly bracket) to be treated as simple text.

}(close curly bracket)   Enables the special macro character (the close curly bracket) to be treated as simple text.

/ *or* < (slash *or* caret)   Displays the 1-2-3 Main Menu.

{ABS [*num*]}   Simulates the F4 key press, optionally repeating F4 *num* times.

{APP1}   Simulates the Alt-F7 key press, invoking any Add-In program attached to that key.

{APP2}   Simulates the Alt-F8 key press, invoking any Add-In program attached to that key.

{APP3}   Simulates the Alt-F9 key press, invoking any Add-In program attached to that key.

{APP4}   Simulates the Alt-F10 key press, invoking any Add-In program attached to that key.

{APPENDBELOW *target,source*}   Copies a *source* range to the range of cells just below a specified *target* range.

{APPENDRIGHT *target,source*}   Copies a *source* range to the range of cells just to the right of a specified *target* range.

{BACKSPACE *[num]*}** *or* **{BS** *[num]*}**   Simulates pressing the Backspace key (←), optionally repeating the keystroke *num* times.

{BEEP *[num]*}**   Sounds your computer's bell, optionally selecting from four possible frequencies. *Num* should range from 1 to 4, with 1 assumed if no entry is made.

{BIGLEFT *[num]*}**   Simulates the Ctrl-← or Shift-Tab key press, optionally repeating the keystroke *num* times.

{BIGRIGHT *[num]*}**   Simulates the Ctrl-→ or Tab key press, optionally repeating the keystroke *num* times.

{BLANK *location*}**   Erases the contents of the cell or range specified by *location*. This macro is comparable to the /Range Erase command, but is faster because no recalculations occur.

{BORDERSOFF}   Clears row numbers and column letters from the screen during a macro's execution.

{BORDERSON}   Redisplays row numbers and column letters from the screen that were previously hidden during a macro's execution.

{BRANCH *location*}**   Transfers execution control from within one macro to the instructions found directly at *location.*

{BREAK}   Restores 1-2-3 to Ready mode at the beginning of a macro to ensure a consistent starting state for subsequent macro instructions.

{BREAKOFF}   Turns off 1-2-3 recognition of the Ctrl-Break key press. This macro keeps users from interrupting an executing macro.

{BREAKON}   Restores the user's ability to interrupt an executing macro with the Ctrl-Break key press.

{CALC *[num]*}**   Simulates the F9 key press, optionally repeating the keystroke *num* times. In Ready mode, {CALC} recalculates all worksheet formulas. In Value or Edit mode, {CALC} replaces a formula with its current value.

{CLOSE}   Closes an open text file. Subsequent instructions in the same macro cell are ignored, and execution continues with the instruction in the next cell.

{CONTENTS *target,source,[width],[format]*}   Copies a value from *source,* or the top-left cell of *source,* and converts it to a label before rewriting it in the *target* location. *Width* and *format* enforce specified characteristics to the resulting *target* cell.

{DEFINE *loc1,loc2,…,locn*}   Indicates the cell locations to use for storing input arguments to a subroutine. Each *loc* entry can have a :S or :V suffix to define whether the argument is a string (the default) or a value.

{DELETE *[num]*} *or* **{DEL** *[num]*}   Simulates the Del key press, optionally repeating the keystroke *num* times.

{DISPATCH *location*}   Transfers execution control from within one macro to the instructions found indirectly, by using the address or range name found in *location.*

{DOWN *[num]*} *or* **{D** *[num]*}   Simulates the ↓ key, optionally repeating the keystroke *num* times.

{EDIT}   Simulates the F2 key press.

{END}   Simulates the End key press.

{ESCAPE *[num]*} *or* **{ESC** *[num]*}   Simulates the Esc key press, optionally repeating the keystroke *num* times.

{FILESIZE *location*}   Counts the number of bytes in the currently open text file and enters that value in the cell specified by *location.*

{FOR *counter,start,stop,step,subroutine*}   Repeats a *subroutine* a number of times, tracked by *counter* which begins with a value of *start,* increments by *step,* and ends when *counter* exceeds a value of *stop.*

{FORBREAK}   Cancels an executing FOR subroutine.

{FORM *location,[call-table],[include-list | exclude-list]*}
Pauses a macro to allow data to be entered or edited in unprotected cells in the input range specified by *location.* Similar to but more flexible than the /Range Input command, this macro allows you to define a *call-table* that specifies macro

actions to perform when special keys are pressed. You can also include or exclude certain keystrokes during this processing.

{FORMBREAK}   Cancels an executing {FORM} macro instruction.

{FRAMEOFF}   Clears row numbers and column letters from the screen during a macro's execution.

{FRAMEON}   Redisplays row numbers and column letters on the screen that were previously hidden during a macro's execution.

{GET *location*}   Pauses a macro until you press a single key. 1-2-3 stores the keystroke in *location* as a label.

{GETLABEL *prompt,location*}   Pauses a macro, displays *prompt* in the control panel, and stores the typed response as a left-aligned label in *location.*

{GETNUMBER *prompt,location*}   Pauses a macro, displays *prompt* in the control panel, and stores the typed response as a value in *location.*

{GETPOS *location*}   Obtains the current positional value of the byte pointer in the open text file, storing this value in *location.*

{GOTO}   Simulates the F5 key press.

{GRAPH}   Simulates the F10 key press, displaying the current worksheet graph.

{GRAPHOFF}   Restores the worksheet screen after a graph has been displayed.

{GRAPHON *[named-graph],[nodisplay]*}   Displays a *named graph* or the current worksheet graph, or simply makes a named graph current without displaying it.

{HELP}   Simulates the F1 key press, displaying context-sensitive help information.

{HOME}   Simulates the Home key press.

{IF *condition*}   Performs the remaining macro instruction in the current cell, if *condition* is logically true; otherwise, continues executing with the first instruction in the next cell in the macro's column.

{INDICATE *[string]*}   Displays *string* as a new mode indicator in the upper-right corner of your screen, or restores 1-2-3's mode indicators (when a *string* entry is not included), or clears the mode indicator completely (when " " is used as the *string*).

{INSERT} *or* **{INS}**   Simulates the Ins key press.

{LEFT *[num]*} or **{L** *[num]*}   Simulates the ← key press, optionally repeating the keystroke *num* times.

{LET *location,entry*}   Evaluates *entry,* storing the result in *location.*

{LOOK *location*}   Reads the keyboard type-ahead buffer, storing the first keystroke as a label in *location.*

{MENU}   Displays the 1-2-3 Main Menu.

{MENUBRANCH *location*}   Displays in the control panel a macro menu found at *location.* The macro waits for a selection and branches unconditionally to the instructions associated with the selected menu choice.

{MENUCALL *location*}   Displays in the control panel a macro menu found at *location.* The macro waits for a selection and executes a subroutine associated with the selected menu choice.

{NAME}   Simulates the F3 key press.

{ONERROR *action-loc,[message-loc]*}   Traps errors during macro execution, storing the error message in *message-loc* and branching to *action-loc* for subsequent error handling.

{OPEN *filename,access*}   Makes a text file available to your worksheet for reading or writing. *Access* determines whether the connection is read-only (R), modify (M), or append (A) for existing files, or write/read (W) for new files.

{PANELOFF *[clear]*}   Stops automatic entry by 1-2-3 into the control panel and status line, and optionally erases these lines first.

{PANELON}   Restores the control panel and status line to normal display operations.

{PGDN *[num]*}   Simulates the PgDn (Page Down) key press, optionally repeating the keystroke *num* times.

{PGUP *[num]*}   Simulates the PgUp (Page Up) key press, optionally repeating the keystroke *num* times.

{PUT *location,column,row,entry*}   Stores a 1-2-3 string or value *entry* into a range identified by *location.* The cell that receives the *entry* is specified by the relative *column* and *row* offsets (beginning with 0) into the range.

{QUERY}   Simulates the F7 key press.

{QUIT}   Immediately terminates an executing macro.

{READ *bytes,location*}   Copies a requested number of *bytes* from an open text file, storing them as a label at *location*.

{READLN *location*}   Copies a line of text from the open text file to *location*.

{RECALC *location,[condition],[iterations]*}   Recalculates all formulas in *location*, proceeding through the cells in the range from left to right each row, moving successively from the top row to the bottom one. Optionally, repeats the recalculation a fixed number of *iterations* or until a *condition* becomes true.

{RECALCCOL *location,[condition],[iterations]*}   Recalculates all formulas in *location*, proceeding through the cells in the range from top to bottom in each column, moving successively from the leftmost column to the rightmost one. Optionally, repeats the recalculation a fixed number of *iterations* or until a *condition* becomes true.

{RESTART}   Clears the subroutine stack of return addresses so that the macro ends when the final current subroutine instruction executes.

{RETURN}   Transfers control back to a calling location. This macro is used at the end of a {SUBROUTINE} or {MENUCALL} macro.

{RIGHT *[num]*} *or* {R *[num]*}   Simulates the → key press, optionally repeating the keystroke *num* times.

{SETPOS *offset*}   Sets the position *offset* (with respect to position 0) of an open text file's byte pointer.

{SUBROUTINE *[arg1],[arg2],...*}   Executes a previously defined subroutine, optionally transferring one or more arguments to the routine.

{SYSTEM *command*}   Runs an operating system *command*, then continues executing the current macro.

{TABLE}   Simulates the F8 key press.

{UP *[num]*} *or* {U *[num]*}   Simulates the ↑ key press, optionally repeating the keystroke *num* times.

{**WAIT** *time-number*}   Pauses a macro until the system time reaches the specified *time-number*.

{**WINDOW**}   Simulates the F6 key press.

{**WINDOWSOFF**}   Speeds up macro execution by suppressing all screen updates until a {WINDOWSON} command or the macro completes.

{**WINDOWSON**}   Restores normal screen updating during macro processing.

{**WRITE** *string*}   Copies a *string* of text to the currently open text file, beginning at the current byte pointer position.

{**WRITELN** *string*}   Copies a *string* of text to the currently open text file, beginning at the current byte pointer position, and terminates the string with a carriage return and line feed sequence.

/X MACRO COMMAND EQUIVALENTS

The /X macro commands in Table A.1 appeared in 1-2-3 Release 1A. Release 2.3 and 2.4 can process them, but their full keyword equivalents in the current release are easier to read and understand.

Table A.1: 1-2-3 Release 2.3/2.4 Macro Equivalents to Release 1A /X Macro Commands

Release 1A Command	Release 2.3/2.4 Macro Equivalent
/XC	SUBROUTINE
/XG	BRANCH
/XI	IF
/XL	GETLABEL
/XM	MENUBRANCH
/XN	GETNUMBER
/XQ	QUIT
/XR	RETURN

INDEX

D

W

ORDER FORM

If you found this 1-2-3 Instant Reference useful, you'll be glad to learn that every one of the example techniques demonstrated in this book is available in a companion diskette. The diskette contains more than one-hundred demonstration worksheets. Save time, energy, and money ... and avoid the drudgery of typing the many example techniques found in this book.

Use the order form below to obtain the diskette, which was produced by the author, Judd Robbins. Send a money-order or a check *drawn on a United States bank* with complete payment to Judd Robbins, P.O. Box 9656, Berkeley, CA 94709.

SYBEX is not affiliated with this product and assumes no responsibility for any defect in the disk or its contents.

A. 1-2-3 Instant Reference   @ $24.95   = _____
    Companion Disk

B. Shipping and Handling   @ $3.00   = _____
    (foreign orders)   @ US$8.00

C. California Sales Tax @ 7%   = _____

                 TOTAL ORDER: = _____

Specify Disk Format: ☐   3½"   ☐   5¼"

NAME: _____

COMPANY: _____

ADDRESS : _____

CITY, STATE, ZIP : _____

TELEPHONE: _____

SMARTICONS

Icons in Graphics Mode	Icons in Text Mode	Purpose
	Z→A	Sorts a database in descending order.
	+ROW	Inserts one or more worksheet rows.
	+COL	Inserts one or more worksheet columns.
	−ROW	Deletes one or more worksheet rows.
	−COL	Deletes one or more worksheet columns.
		Moves the cell pointer to the A1 Home position.
		Moves the cell pointer to the lower-right corner of the active area.
		Same as END-↓.
		Same as END-↑.
		Same as END-→.
		Same as END-←.
	CALC	Recalculates the worksheet.
	DATE	Enters the system date in the current cell.
	+	Specifies the cell to which to link or reference.
	REP	Replicates the current cell contents in an entire range.
	FMT	Replicates the current cell format in all cells of a range.
	GOTO	Moves the cell pointer to a specified cell.